30 DAYS OF PRAYER

A BIBLE STUDY IN PSALMS

PROVERBS 31 MINISTRIES

FOREWORD BY LYSA TERKEURST

HarperChristian Resources

30 Days of Prayer: A Bible Study in Psalms

Published in Grand Rapids, Michigan, by HarperChristian Resources. HarperChristian Resources is a registered trademark of HarperCollins Christian Publishing, Inc.

Requests for information should be sent to customercare@harpercollins.com.

ISBN 978-0-310-17866-8 (softcover)
ISBN 978-0-310-17867-5 (ebook)

HarperChristian Resources titles may be purchased in bulk for church, business, fundraising, or ministry use. For information, please e-mail ResourceSpecialist@ChurchSource.com.

First Printing July 2025 / Printed in the United States of America

WRITTEN BY PROVERBS 31 STAFF
AND THE FIRST FIVE WRITING TEAM

Shelby Dixon, Claire Foxx, Eric Gagnon, Shae Hill, Joel Muddamalle,
Michaela Roscoe, Meghan Ryan, Lysa TerKeurst, and Glynnis Whitwer

Quantrilla Ard, Mei Au, Jackie Smith-Bell, Mary Boswell, Kelley Brown, Bronwyn Cardwell,
Kellye Schiffner Carver, Andrea Chatelain, Lyli Dunbar, Karen Ehman, Kayla Ferris,
Sarah Frazer, Trisha Hawk, Marissa Henley, Sandy Johnson, Micah Maddox,
Catherine Martinez, Katy McCown, Lisa Alvin-Meyer, Jodie Nizkik,
Denise Pass, Melanie Davis Porter, Bethany Ruth, Sandell Snyder,
Melissa Spoelstra, Erica Wiggenhorn, Joy A Williams

"PRAY CONTINUALLY"

ERIC GAGNON

That's what God's Word tells us to do in 1 Thessalonians 5:17. It's one of the shortest, simplest verses in the Bible, but if we're honest ... doesn't it seem kind of impossible?

What if your prayers feel like attempts to fill the silence in one-way conversations with a God who hears but seemingly never speaks?

What if you're used to asking God for help in hard seasons, but you're not sure what to talk to Him about the rest of the time?

What if you feel close to the Lord at church, but when you want to pray worshipful words on your own, it's not the same?

What if you finally set aside a whole hour to talk to God, but after a few minutes, your thoughts wander — then you feel guilty, so you press your palms together and close your eyes tighter and try to pray about how you wish you could pray better?

We're with you, friend. We've spent midnights staring at the ceiling and wondering why the God of the universe would even listen to what we have to say. Like you, we have journals full of questions, prayer requests and half-finished confessions interrupted by crying children, and our calendars have "prayer time" written in and then erased (more than once).

But what if ... prayer isn't meant to be this complicated?

The book of Psalms in the Old Testament is filled with prayers God has graciously given us to show *it is possible* to pray continually — but only if we let go of our impossible ideas about how we're "supposed to" feel, what we're "supposed to" say, and where we're "supposed to" be when we come to Him.

As we study Psalms, we'll be stunned by the writers' freedom of expression: Some psalms are long and poetic, but others are shorter than a TV commercial. Some are prayers of joyful praise and gratitude, but others are miserable complaints — and many are both. Some prayers are directly connected to what the psalmists were experiencing, and other times the psalmists chose not to focus on their circumstances but instead looked to the transcendent. They talked to God about the past, and they talked to Him about the future, and they asked Him for strength and forgiveness and rescue and justice in the present.

Psalm 42:1 says, *"As the deer pants for streams of water, so my soul pants for you, my God."* And here's the thing: Drinking water when we're thirsty doesn't feel like work. It isn't exhausting, inconvenient or stressful, and we don't need formal education or special skills to do it. Maybe prayer is the same way — it's not just something we're supposed to give *to* God but a way of receiving *from* Him everything we need. More than a continual challenge, prayer is a continual calling into deeper, sweeter, life-sustaining abiding with our heavenly Father.

What a relief!

We pray this study will be a blessing to you as we reflect on the psalms God has given us to guide our prayers — and we hope you'll also enjoy hearing from Proverbs 31 Ministries' Director of Theological Research, Dr. Joel Muddamalle, along the way as we learn, grow and pray together.

Welcome to *30 Days of Prayer: A Bible Study in Psalms.*

— Claire, Eric, Glynnis, Joel, Meghan, Michaela, Shae and Shelby

WHAT IS PRAYER?

THE SIMPLEST DEFINITION OF PRAYER IS "COMMUNICATION WITH GOD."

BUT WHAT DOES THAT LOOK LIKE?

- "Communication with God, primarily offered in the second-person voice (addressing God directly). May include petition, entreaty, supplication, thanksgiving, praise, hymns, and lament."[1]
- "Though prayer also includes adoration ... Christian prayer has always been essentially petitionary."[2]
- "The addressing and petitioning of God."[3]
- "The activity of bringing all our desires and thanksgiving to God with full humility and submission to his will, confident that God will hear and respond."[4]
- "Dialogue between God and people, especially His covenant partners."[5]

If some of these terms are difficult, don't worry! The point is how scholars vary in defining something so simple yet also very deep. This study is all about uncomplicating prayer — so we'll dig into what it means to do things like "petition" and "supplicate" (ways of presenting requests to God) as we study thirty psalms in the next six weeks. But for now, it's worth noting that all of these definitions share the idea that prayer is a form of communication from God's people to God Himself.

As we mentioned in the welcome letter to this study, God's Word tells us to *"pray continually"* (1 Thessalonians 5:17). Some have taken this verse to mean we don't need to spend any specific time or even use words to pray; we simply pray all day as we think about God and what we need.

For instance, this idea is reflected in a poem by James Montgomery:

> Prayer is the soul's sincere desire,
> Unuttered or expressed;
> The motion of a hidden fire
> That trembles in the breast.
>
> Prayer is the burden of a sigh,
> The falling of a tear
> The upward glancing of an eye,
> When none but God is near.[6]

Certainly our upward glances may be counted as a beginning of prayer ... but prayer is also much more than that, according to God's Word. Sometimes our prayers may be simple expressions of emotions to God, but other times they may be more conversational. As we grow in our experience and confidence in prayer, we may even see our prayers change.

Many cultures and religions throughout history speak about communication with their gods — gods who sit in high, unreachable places, who must be begged and appeased to speak and be spoken to. But the God of the Bible, Yahweh, (Exodus 3:14) is unique in that He invites us to communicate with Him!

He says our prayers are like a pleasing aroma to Him. (Psalm 141:2; Revelation 5:8) And not only this — He speaks to *us* in His Word, and He shows us the very prayers He loves to answer! What an amazing God we have.

WHY PRAY THE PSALMS?

If prayer is communication with God, then the ancient songs of the people sung to God are also prayers. Poetry written to and about God is prayer. The biblical psalms, then, are all a form of prayer.

We can pray with *confidence* through the psalms knowing that when we pray them, we are praying alongside authors who prayed in God's inspired will.

THE GENRES OF THE PSALMS SPEAK FOR OUR EVERY NEED

Praise
Confession
Thanksgiving
Lament
Trust
Wisdom
Intercession *and* supplication

First John 5:14-15 says, *"This is the confidence we have in approaching God: that if we ask anything according to his will, he hears us. And if we know that he hears us—whatever we ask—we know that we have what we asked of him."*

Praying the psalms gives us a massive amount of words to pray when we can't find words on our own. There is certainty when we pray the words of Scripture back to God. We come to trust if God's answer is "no," it is also a "yes" or "wait" for something better.

Examples of Psalms Likely Influencing New Testament Prayers

In the following verses from Matthew, Mark, Luke, John and Acts, the prayers spoken by God's people so closely resemble the language of psalms that theologians suspect psalms were the inspiration. (Or in the case of Jesus, He was fulfilling psalms.) Spend a few moments comparing some of these verses:

NEW TESTAMENT PRAYER	SOME SHARED LANGUAGE/IDEAS	PSALMS
Matthew 11:25 (A prayer of Jesus)		Psalm 8:2
John 17:6; John 17:26 (A prayer of Jesus)		Psalm 22:22
John 17:12 (A prayer of Jesus)		Psalm 109:8
Luke 23:46 (A prayer of Jesus)		Psalm 31:5
Matthew 6:10 (A prayer of Jesus)		Psalm 103:21
Matthew 27:46 (A prayer of Jesus)		Psalm 22:1
Luke 1:46-55 (Mary's Song)		Psalm 34:2-3,10; Psalm 35:9; Psalm 69:30; Psalm 71:19; Psalm 72:17; Psalm 75:7; Psalm 89:1-2, 8, 10
Acts 4:23-31 (A prayer of Peter and John)		Psalm 2:1-2; Psalm 102:25; Psalm 124:8; Psalm 134:3; Psalm 138:7; Psalm 146:6
Acts 7:59 (A prayer of Stephen)		Psalm 31:5

How To Build a Habit of Prayer

Knowing that God wants us to communicate with Him, we might ask: When? Where? How do we build a habit of prayer?

The Bible gives us a lot of freedom in answering that question, but it's clear God wants us to pray. God didn't create prayer as a chore we have to do, feeling guilty when we fail; it's an active conversation He invites us into.

Prayer is something we *get* to do as believers in Christ.

Where do we find motivation and power to pray?

ROMANS 8:9

You, however, are not in the realm of the flesh but are in the realm of the Spirit, if indeed the Spirit of God lives in you.

Remember that at that time you were separate from Christ.

EPHESIANS 2:12

1 TIMOTHY 2:5-6

For there is one God and one mediator between God and mankind, the man Christ Jesus, who gave himself as a ransom for all people.

And I will do whatever you ask in my name.

JOHN 14:13

JAMES 5:16b

The prayer of a righteous person is powerful and effective.

For the mouth speaks what the heart is full of.

MATTHEW 12:34

How do we learn to love God more so that we pray more?

Here's one way: Jesus said, *"whoever has been forgiven little loves little"* (Luke 7:47b). This also implies that he or she who is forgiven much, loves much. If we know we are wicked, broken sinners saved by God's grace alone and not by anything good in ourselves, then we know God's amazing love for us — and in return, we love Him all the more.

David, the man God used to record most of the prayers in the book of Psalms, was well acquainted with his own wickedness and the forgiveness he received from God. After Nathan confronted David for adultery and murder, although there would be significant consequences:

Then David said to Nathan, "I have sinned against the Lord."

Nathan replied, "The Lord has taken away your sin. You are not going to die." (2 Samuel 12:13)

This was tremendous grace, especially since this happened during a time when Israel was governed by the old covenant of the law.

To understand the depth of our sin, we also study God's law. We read the Ten Commandments in Exodus 20. We study His holiness. Like a mirror, God's law shows us how utterly short we fall of being worthy of eternal life. (Isaiah 6:5) But when we reject our life of rebellion and turn to Him, He runs to us with open arms and receives us as His children just like the father received his prodigal son in Luke 15:11-32.

It's at that point we begin to reflect Jesus Himself and rise early in the morning to pray. We take joy in fasting and praying like Jesus did in the wilderness. (Matthew 4:1-4) We pray into the night like He did in the garden of Gethsemane. (Matthew 26:36-46) We do as David and Daniel did and praythroughout the day. (Psalm 119:164; Daniel 6:10) Our passion for being in relationship with God fuels our prayers.

What does this mean for today? Where do we start?

Some days we have less time to pray than others. However and whenever we pray, it is clear from Scripture that we are called to pray *frequently*.

Church reformer Martin Luther was known to have said, "I have so much to do today that I shall spend the first three hours in prayer."[1]

NOTE FROM JOEL
USE YOUR WORDS IN PRAYER

Getting into the habit of verbally relating and communicating with God is a practice of reinforcing truths about God and who we are in light of God. To say that our words frame our reality is to acknowledge that what comes out of our mouths usually indicates what is present deep within our hearts. Making a commitment to use words in our prayers is multifaceted:

1. We learn from Scripture what words to use.

2. We can consider the words that flow out of our mouths to help us consider the condition of our hearts.

3. We may find that the honest words we pray will define what we truly need to pray for.

Maybe you haven't prayed daily in a long time — or ever — and if so, you're not alone! We're in this together. You can start today, right where you are: The Lord's Prayer in Matthew 6, just four sentences long, shows us that God is honored by even a short prayer. (To learn more about this, flip to "Praying the Lord's Prayer" on page 213.)

Or maybe you struggle with wanting to pray regularly because you know God is in control and does all He pleases.

Our God is in heaven;
   he does whatever pleases him. (Psalm 115:3)

It may help to remember that throughout Scripture, God is pleased to work and act *after* prayer (e.g., 2 Chronicles 33:12-13; Numbers 14:13-20; Mark 9:25-29; Acts 9:40-41). In the very act of praying, you are writing a part of the history of how God loves to move, act and answer. It pleases God for it to be so.

We hope this study of praying in the psalms will help you continue to build a habit of daily praying *"on all occasions with all kinds of prayers and requests"* (Ephesians 6:18). It is our prayer that in the years to come, you'll look back and see how God strengthened you so that you might, *"in every situation, by prayer and petition, with thanksgiving, present your requests to God"* (Philippians 4:6).

Notes on the Psalms

- The book of Psalms is divided into 150 chapters, which contain a total of roughly 2,500 verses. It is the third-longest book in the Bible, containing somewhere around 30,147 words, preceded by Genesis in second place (32,046 words) and Jeremiah in first place (33,002 words).[1]
- Psalms 1, 42, 73, 90 and 107 start with a doxology — a praise to God for His Word or His goodness — each introducing a new section in the book.
- There are five 'books' or sections within the book of Psalms.
- Psalms has more named authors than any other book of the Bible. These include: David, the sons of Korah, Moses, Asaph, Solomon, Heman the Ezrahite and Ethan the Ezrahite. Additionally, many psalms are anonymous.
- Five psalms are actually titled "A Prayer": Psalms 17, 86, 90, 102 and 142.
- Church father Athanasius said, "The Psalms have a unique place in the Bible because whereas most of Scripture speaks to us, the Psalm speak for us."[2]

WHAT YOU HAVE TO LOOK FORWARD TO IN THIS STUDY

Daily Teachings and Reflection Questions
Each week of this study includes daily teachings on five biblical psalms. We'll work through how each psalm helps us uncomplicate our prayer lives today. The daily questions and reflections will guide your personal prayer time and study.

Psalm Annotation Exercises
For our fifth day of study each week, we'll include the full text of one psalm and invite you to take notes and mark up the text alongside us as we look at the words and images of the Scriptures in depth.

Praying a Psalm
We will use a psalm from our study to pray God's Word back to Him. This will be our exercise in habit forming and where we will come to see how generously God has given us the very words our hearts long to speak, in need and in praise.

Weekend Reflection and Prayer
Each weekend, we'll summarize some important ideas we've learned throughout the week and close with a prayer.

Bonus Content
Sprinkled throughout this guide, you'll also find some special insights and notes from Proverbs 31 Ministries' Director of Theological Research, Dr. Joel Muddamalle! Occasionally we'll also dive into a Hebrew word study, explore the relationship between prayer and our emotions, learn about how Jesus prays for us, and more.

Praying the Lord's Prayer
At the end of our study, we've included an additional resource you can use to pray like Jesus did in Matthew 6, using the Lord's Prayer to shape your own conversations with God.

TABLE OF CONTENTS

WEEK 4
Prayers of Lament

DAY 16 (PSALM 102)
For the woman who needs to say she's not OK.

DAY 17 (PSALM 10)
For the woman who doesn't know how to pray when it seems like evil is winning.

DAY 18 (PSALM 90)
For the woman who needs a way to grieve with hope.

DAY 19 (PSALM 22)
For the woman who needs to know she's not alone.

DAY 20 (PSALM 142)
For the woman who is desperate for a safe place.

WEEK 5
Prayers of Supplication

DAY 21 (PSALM 37)
For the woman who needs to be reminded she can talk to God about anything.

DAY 22 (PSALM 17)
For the woman who longs to be delivered out of the hardship she's facing.

DAY 23 (PSALM 143)
For the woman who is asking God, What's next? Where do I go from here?

DAY 24 (PSALM 31)
For the woman who is continuing to pray even when her circumstances haven't changed.

DAY 25 (PSALM 121)
For the woman who is placing her hope in the helping hands of God.

WEEK 6
Prayers of Intercession

DAY 26 (PSALM 106)
For the woman who needs the reminder that redemption is always possible.

DAY 27 (PSALM 60)
For the woman who needs God to do what she can't do for the people she loves.

DAY 28 (PSALM 20)
For the woman whose loved ones are facing a battle.

DAY 29 (PSALM 28)
For the woman who needs confidence that the Lord will carry her and her people.

DAY 30 (PSALM 33)
For the woman who wants to celebrate what God has done in her and her loved ones' lives.

FOREWORD BY LYSA TERKEURST

Early in the morning, my sleepy eyes beg me to stay in bed a little longer.

But my soul stirs to get up and talk with Jesus.

It's not always easy to prioritize time with God.
It's not always perfectly quiet or undistracted.
It's not always for a long, extended period of time.

But I know time set aside with God prepares me for what I will need throughout the day. It's the time where He equips me to handle what is ahead with His gentle boldness, quiet strength and loving grace. And though I can't physically see Him, I know He is present.

Many times when I open my Bible, I find myself in the psalms and pray through the verses. As I do, a beautiful melody of God's truth rises up and my worries fade in their light. His perspective on what troubles me overshadows my anxiety.

In Psalm 81:10b, God instructs, *"Open wide your mouth and I will fill it."* This reminds me that He will give me what to say. What to say in happy moments and in aggravating moments. What to say when I feel insecure and what to say when I am confident. He also reminds me that sometimes it is good to say nothing at all as the Holy Spirit guides me in self-control.

Psalm 84:1 reminds me that God's dwelling place is "lovely". So, I ask for Him to dwell in me richly. I want it to be evident that I'm a girl who spends time with Jesus and that He's working on me.

Psalm 86:11 prompts me to ask, *"Teach me your way, LORD, that I may rely on your faithfulness; give me an undivided heart, that I may fear your name."* I want my heart to be undivided. I want to be drawn toward faith, not distracted by fear. I want to be drawn toward trusting the Lord, not tempted to try and control things beyond my ability to control. I want to be drawn toward the peace Jesus gives, not constantly confused by the chaos of the world.

Each of these verses leads me to a prayer I've been praying for years:

God, I want to see You.
God, I want to hear You.
God, I want to know You.
God, I want to follow hard after You.

And I know...
God, You are good.
You are good to me.
You are good at being God.

Therefore, today, I trade my will for Thy will because I'm so assured that You will.

Oh friend, we must exchange whispers with God before shouts with the world. I don't always do this perfectly, but getting just a little more intentional about prayer has made it a greater daily rhythm in my life.

That's why I'm so glad you picked up this Bible study.

Be assured: the book of Psalms was not written by perfect people in perfect circumstances. No, it's filled with real words, cried out by real people, sometimes in real times of hardship. The psalmists remind us to not isolate ourselves during our own difficult circumstances but instead to dig into gut-honest conversations with God.

And that's what the next thirty days is all about.

Whether you feel invigorated in your faith or discouraged by unanswered prayers, *God is here.* My hope and prayer is that you experience His presence in a real way through these pages. Not because everything is or will be perfect, but because He is good.

Many Blessings,

WEEK ONE

PRAYERS OF ADORATION

A psalm of praise. Of David.

1 I will exalt you, my God the King;
I will praise your name for ever and ever.
2 Every day I will praise you
and extol your name for ever and ever.

3 Great is the LORD and most worthy of praise;
his greatness no one can fathom.
4 One generation commends your works to another;
they tell of your mighty acts.
5 They speak of the glorious splendor of your majesty—
and I will meditate on your wonderful works.
6 They tell of the power of your awesome works—
and I will proclaim your great deeds.
7 They celebrate your abundant goodness
and joyfully sing of your righteousness.

8 The LORD is gracious and compassionate,
slow to anger and rich in love.

9 The LORD is good to all;
he has compassion on all he has made.
10 All your works praise you, LORD;
your faithful people extol you.
11 They tell of the glory of your kingdom
and speak of your might,
12 so that all people may know of your mighty acts
and the glorious splendor of your kingdom.
13 Your kingdom is an everlasting kingdom,
and your dominion endures through all generations.

The LORD is trustworthy in all he promises
and faithful in all he does.
14 The LORD upholds all who fall
and lifts up all who are bowed down.
15 The eyes of all look to you,
and you give them their food at the proper time.
16 You open your hand
and satisfy the desires of every living thing.

17 The LORD is righteous in all his ways
and faithful in all he does.
18 The LORD is near to all who call on him,
to all who call on him in truth.
19 He fulfills the desires of those who fear him;
he hears their cry and saves them.
20 The LORD watches over all who love him,
but all the wicked he will destroy.
21 My mouth will speak in praise of the LORD.
Let every creature praise his holy name
for ever and ever.

DAY 1

In the Light of His Glory and Grace

For the woman who wants to know God but doubts that it's possible.

GLYNNIS WHITWER AND KAYLA FERRIS

TODAY'S READING: Psalm 145

MAJOR MOMENT: David praised God's greatness.

KEY VERSE: Psalm 145:6

They tell of the power of your awesome works—
and I will proclaim your great deeds.

There is an old hymn, written in the early 20th century by Helen Lemmel, that reminds us to turn our eyes upon Jesus and "look full in His wonderful face." It goes on to say that by doing this, we'll see the "things of earth will grow strangely dim in the light of His glory and grace."

Indeed, there is something that happens when we see and know and declare who God is. We gain a proper perspective on everything else.

As we begin our prayer journey through the book of Psalms, it's right, but maybe not entirely natural, that we start with prayers of adoration or praise.

When we start to pray, it's so easy to move quickly to thanksgiving or requests — depending on the day and what we've been through. And sometimes a quick "emergency prayer" is all we can manage. But the psalmists invite us to back up a bit and pause ... take a breath ... and focus on the One we love and serve.

Adoring God is different than being thankful for Him. Adoration is praise that originates from our hearts and that we pour out on God. It's a declaration and elevation of His character and acts. Thanksgiving is our response to the love, blessing and compassion that flows from God onto us.

When we pause to praise God in prayer, it repositions our hearts. And as we refocus on who God is, we are reminded that no matter what we face today, God is bigger than our circumstances. Praise magnifies God to the position He deserves in our lives, and our problems diminish in light of His majesty.

Adoration is *praise* that originates from our hearts and that we *pour out on God.*

So today we'll look at Psalm 145, the only biblical psalm actually subtitled "A Song of Praise." In fact, Psalms 145-150 have been called the "grand doxology of the entire collection" of psalms, as these six psalms focus on praise.[1]

Verse 3 clearly and simply declares why praise is important: *"Great is the LORD and most worthy of praise; his greatness no one can fathom."*

Prayers of adoration are easier to pray when we know more about God's greatness. Psalm 145 demonstrates how King David, *"a man after [God's] own heart"* (1 Samuel 13:14), knew God intimately. David understood God's character and had personally witnessed many of God's acts of faithfulness and love. David's words of adoration are a declaration of these truths. His knowledge of God led to worshipful prayer, and this worship gave him perspective.

Even if we haven't experienced God in all the ways described in this psalm, we can learn about God through David's praise. This is merely the beginning of how the psalms are so helpful as we learn how to pray.

In verses 4-7, we see that God's people passed down testimonies of His actions through the generations. These faithful actions are reasons to praise God.

How does David describe God's actions in verses 4-7?

These verses speak of a God who acts, and what He *does* always perfectly reflects who He *is*. He is not an absent God. He is not disconnected from His people. He is observant and engaged.

In what ways has God acted on your behalf or your family's behalf?

As we work through this study, we will see the power of praying God's words back to Him, as King David demonstrates in verse 8. This verse includes one of the most-quoted sayings in the Old Testament, first spoken by God to Moses on Mount Sinai as God was preparing the second set of tablets containing the Ten Commandments. (Exodus 34:6) These special words weren't just ascribed to God by humans; God declared this about *Himself.*

Write Psalm 145:8 below and circle the descriptors of God that most stand out to you as worthy of adoration. Of these characteristics, which ones do you most need to experience today? Why?

By declaring God's grace and mercy, David reminds us that when we turn our eyes to God's greatness, the weight of the world slides off us (Psalm 145:8-9).

NOTE FROM JOEL

When we participate in praying Scripture back to God, we are actually entering into an ancient practice that was common among the people of God. The remembrance of scriptures in order to repeat them plays an important part in helping us see how the Bible is cohesive and unified. Here's a little "pro tip" as you read your Bible: Sometimes there will be footnotes or a middle column that has a bunch of other verses listed. These are called "cross-references," and they show us where certain words or thoughts appear elsewhere throughout the Bible.

Starting with Psalm 145:14, we find a series of beautiful descriptions of a caring heavenly Father attuned to the needs of His children. As we look more closely at who God helps, we see His compassion toward those who are hurting, fallen, needy and afraid.

If that's you today, take comfort in knowing your Father sees you and knows what you need. And as we have learned today, He is a God who acts on His children's behalf.

Describe God's character in your own words from what you read in verses 14-20.

Indeed, there is something that happens when we see and know and declare who God is. We gain a proper perspective on everything else.

As David's life and Psalm 145 illustrate, the more we know God, the more we'll praise God. And the more we declare our adoration of Him, the more perspective we gain as we realize this world is only temporary, but we will praise the Lord for all eternity. Psalm 145 both opens and closes with *"for ever and ever"* praise (Psalm 145:1; Psalm 145:21), creating a kind of infinite prayer loop that ends where it starts and so never really ends: Adoration of God leads to more adoration, which leads to more adoration, which leads to more ...

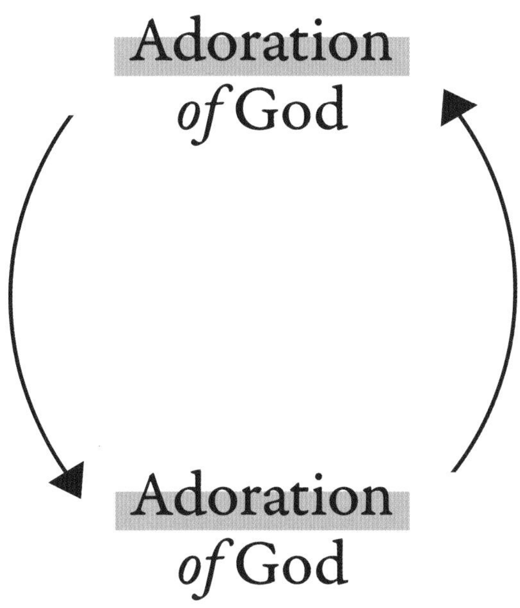

NOTE FROM JOEL
MORE MOMENTS ABOUT PSALM 145

Psalm 145:21 says, *"Let every creature* ***praise his holy name*** *for ever and ever"* (emphasis mine). When it comes to prayer, one of the best ways to begin is by declaring God's holy name! Jesus taught this when He taught His disciples the Lord's Prayer. In Matthew 6:9, He said, *"This, then, is how you should pray: '"Our Father in heaven, hallowed be your name."'"* The ESV Bible says another way to translate *"hallowed be your name"* is *"let your name be kept holy."*

Especially in the Ancient Near Eastern context of Scripture, a name was more than a reference word. A name held meaning. It revealed something of the character of the one it referred to. In Psalm 145, David often used God's covenantal name, *Yahweh* (translated "LORD"), but throughout the Bible, God is described in many other ways too. He is *Jehovah Raah,* the Lord My Shepherd, in Psalm 23:1. He is *Jehovah Rapha,* the Lord Who Heals, in Exodus 15:26. He is *Jehovah Jireh,* the Lord Who Will Provide, in Genesis 22:14. He is *El Roi,* the God of Seeing, in Genesis 16:13. And these are only a few examples.

By referring to the holy names and characteristics of God, we remember and declare who God is. We align our hearts to see His greatness and strength.

We pray to our loving Father, who is high and enthroned in heaven and whose holy name is to be remembered and praised forever and ever. Amen!

PRAYER PRACTICE

Reread Psalm 145. Pay special attention to what you are drawn to most. Use the space below to write the psalm in your own words as a prayer of adoration to the Lord. You needn't write verse by verse, but use God's Word to direct your prayer in structure and theme.

For the director of music. According to gittith. A psalm of David.

1 LORD, our Lord,
how majestic is your name in all the earth!
You have set your glory
in the heavens.
2 Through the praise of children and infants
you have established a stronghold against your enemies,
to silence the foe and the avenger.
3 When I consider your heavens,
the work of your fingers,
the moon and the stars,
which you have set in place,
4 what is mankind that you are mindful of them,
human beings that you care for them?
5 You have made them a little lower than the angels
and crowned them with glory and honor.
6 You made them rulers over the works of your hands;
you put everything under their feet:
7 all flocks and herds,
and the animals of the wild,
8 the birds in the sky,
and the fish in the sea,
all that swim the paths of the seas.
9 LORD, our Lord,
how majestic is your name in all the earth!

DAY 2

God Sees You

For the woman who wonders if God notices her.

GLYNNIS WHITWER AND BRONWYN CARDWELL

TODAY'S READING: Psalm 8

MAJOR MOMENT: God's presence revealed in His creation inspired David to worship Him.

KEY VERSES: Psalm 8:3-4

When I consider your heavens,
the work of your fingers,
the moon and the stars,
which you have set in place,
what is mankind that you are mindful of them,
human beings that you care for them?

We can almost picture a darkened hillside with King David resting on the ground, looking up at the sky, as he wrote Psalm 8 ... the immensity of God's glory and the comparative smallness of humanity brightly illuminated before him.

This psalm is a celebration of awe and wonder, two appropriate responses when we experience the reality of who God is. And adding to the amazement, this same God who is over all creation actually thinks about us!

What a reassuring truth this is for all who feel unseen and overlooked by the artificial light of our world that seems to shine most brightly on a few.

Here in Psalm 8, we are all invited to worship the One who created light and created us. (vv. 3-5) And we find some patterns of praise we can use in our own prayers.

The opening of this psalm expresses the multifaceted relationship we have with God. In verse 1, David first addressed God using His personal name, translated in English as *"Lord"* in all caps. Again, we see intimacy in the use of God's name.

Then David addressed God with what looks to be the same word in English (*"Lord"*) but is translated from a different Hebrew word, *adonai,* meaning "master." Here we see David acknowledge God's dominion and power over all of creation.

> We are all invited to approach God and know Him intimately yet also know Him as Lord over all. Do you find it more comfortable to interact with God as a close friend or as a ruler and leader? Why?

> How has your relationship with the Lord affected your ability to praise Him in prayer?

The size of the universe is incomprehensible. Science makes educated guesses, but according to NASA, the visible universe would take 15 billion light-years to cross.[1]

Seeing God's amazing handiwork in creation caused David to marvel anew that a God so big would concern Himself with seemingly insignificant humans (Psalm 8:3-4).

"What is mankind that you are mindful of them, human beings that you care for them?" (Psalm 8:4)

In Psalm 8:4, David used the word enosh in Hebrew when he said, *"What is* ***mankind*** *that you are mindful of them ... ?"* This word has a connotation of weakness and frailty, indicating the limitations of our human condition.

Why would God care about weak, frail, sinful humans? He cares because He created man and woman in His own image (Genesis 1:27). By giving humankind authority and dominion over the creatures of earth, sea and sky (Genesis 1:28; Psalm 8:6-8), God bestowed honor and favor on those made in His image. And unlike animals and other life on earth, humans can commune with God Himself through prayer, as David's psalm illustrates.

Saying God is *"mindful of [us]"* means we are more than just a passing thought to Him. In other places in Scripture, God remembers His people by acknowledging His promise to them and enacting rescue or help.

Read the following verses and note what you learn about God's remembrance of His people:

Genesis 8:1

Genesis 30:22

Exodus 2:24

Acts 10:30-31

According to theologian Derek Kidner, "Mindful has a compassionately purposeful ring, since God's remembering always implies his movement toward the object of his memory."[2]

What do you learn about God's character by knowing you are on His mind?

We can have confidence that the same God who saw and cared for David sees and cares for each of us. Our lives are not insignificant to Him. First Corinthians 2:9 tells us that we cannot even imagine *"the things God has prepared for those who love him."* We are immensely valuable to God now and for all eternity.

What are your thoughts and prayers today as you consider the greatness of God?

How has He reminded you of His care for you today?

As we wrap up today's study, let's look at verse 5, where the psalmist continues to be in awe of God's creation of humanity: *"You have made them a little lower than the angels and crowned them with glory and honor."*

Although David may not have been thinking of the coming Messiah when he wrote this psalm, his words were prophetic. Hebrews 2:5-8 directly quotes Psalm 8:4-6, referring to Jesus. This passage is followed by an explanation: *"But we do see Jesus, who was made lower than the angels for a little while, now crowned with glory and honor because he suffered death, so that by the grace of God he might taste death for everyone."* (Hebrews 2:9).

By entering our world to become human like us, by overcoming sin through becoming sin for us, Jesus restored the relationship that God intended for us to have with Him. Jesus is now seated *"at God's right hand—with angels, authorities and powers in submission to him"* (1 Peter 3:22). In other words, God has *"put everything under [his] feet"* (Psalm 8:6). All that was intended by God in the creation of humanity was ultimately fulfilled in Jesus Christ.

PRAYER PRACTICE

Take some time to praise God for how He has perfectly revealed His image and character in His Son, Jesus. (Colossians 1:15) List a few things you adore about Him. When you are done, craft a prayer through your list sharing in David's posture of awe and adoration:

PSALM 46

For the director of music. Of the Sons of Korah. According to *alamoth*. A song.

1 God is our refuge and strength,
an ever-present help in trouble.
2 Therefore we will not fear, though the earth give way
and the mountains fall into the heart of the sea,
3 though its waters roar and foam
and the mountains quake with their surging.
4 There is a river whose streams make glad the city of God,
the holy place where the Most High dwells.
5 God is within her, she will not fall;
God will help her at break of day.
6 Nations are in uproar, kingdoms fall;
he lifts his voice, the earth melts.
7 The LORD Almighty is with us;
the God of Jacob is our fortress.
8 Come and see what the LORD has done,
the desolations he has brought on the earth.
9 He makes wars cease
to the ends of the earth.
He breaks the bow and shatters the spear;
he burns the shields with fire.
10 He says, "Be still, and know that I am God;
I will be exalted among the nations,
I will be exalted in the earth."
11 The LORD Almighty is with us;
the God of Jacob is our fortress.

DAY 3

Our Calm in the Chaos

For the woman who needs God to show up in a big way.

GLYNNIS WHITWER AND KELLEY BROWN

TODAY'S READING: Psalm 46

MAJOR MOMENT: The psalmists praised God for being a fortress.

KEY VERSE: Psalm 46:1
God is our refuge and strength,
an ever-present help in trouble.

When our back is against the wall, and the battle we face feels unwinnable ...
When there's not enough in the bank to cover a bill ...
When a relationship is dissolving or our health is at risk ...

These are the times we need God to show up in a big way, and our requests can tumble out in a rapid-fire to-do list.

There's nothing wrong with asking God for help. It shows our faithful trust in Him to act on our behalf.

What if we praised God for what He is able to do rather than just asking Him to do it?

In light of that, we read Psalm 46 today, which gives us words to pray as a battle cry to the One who wins every battle He chooses to fight.

In Psalm 46, the psalmists, the sons of Korah, start by declaring God's power over trouble. We don't know if they were facing something urgent at the moment, but it's interesting that they didn't make any requests of God. We see direct requests in other psalms, but in this one, rather than start with the problem, the psalmists started with the provision: God Himself.

NOTE FROM JOEL

The phrase *"LORD Almighty"* (v. 7) is a militaristic Hebrew phrase and speaks to God as the King of the heavenly army. In Psalm 46, God is the type of King who is on the front line of battle. He alone wields ultimate strength; the King is in total control, and all power flows out from Him. The psalmists compared God to a *"fortress"* (Psalm 46:7; Psalm 46:11); He is indestructible, and He offers us present strength and eternal safety that cannot be found anywhere else.

The psalmists may have been desperate for help, but rather than dissolve into fear, they boldly stated exactly what God is able to do. They declared the Truth of God's character and power in a way that stirred their faith. And we can use this same pattern of praise to stir our faith and prepare our hearts for whatever we face.

What are you facing today, or have you faced in the past, that is/was overwhelming?

What attributes of God would bring you peace today as you face that challenge? Use Psalm 46 as a guide.

Just imagine how much power it would take to make *"wars cease to the ends of the earth"* (Psalm 46:9). That is the power of our God, and that is His plan for eternity! There are countless troubles in the world that threaten our sense of peace and joy today: financial stress, political turmoil, cultural quarrels, natural disasters, diseases, broken relationships and losses of loved ones. But remembering God's mission and His promise to His people encourages our hearts because God already knows how the future will unfold. We don't have to question how the story will end or what our ultimate fate will be.

The confidence of the psalmists is striking in Psalm 46. They imagined the very worst physical catastrophe, if the earth gave way and the sea roared, (vv. 2-3) but calmly testified that even then, we wouldn't need to fear because God would be there.

Isn't this confidence amazing? We can be sure the psalmists' confidence was neither self-generated nor tethered to their ability to save themselves. That would feel very insecure indeed and could lead to fear.

When fear takes over, it's often a sign we are trusting someone or something other than God for help and strength. We trust our jobs for provision or the weather for our safety. But only God is completely dependable. Identify at least one fear you have and what/whom you are trusting other than God.

What steps can you take to *be still* so you can rest in the Lord?

The psalmists praised God with a God-given confidence. This is surely the soul-rest Jesus spoke about in Matthew 11:28-29 when He said: *"Come to me, all you who are weary and burdened, and I will give you rest. Take my yoke upon you and learn from me, for I am gentle and humble in heart, and you will find rest for your souls."*

The only way we will experience this rest for our souls is when our souls rest in God. Psalm 46 invites us to rest in the knowledge that God is in control and shows us how to affirm God's power in prayer. God will show up in times of trouble. The question is: Do we believe it?

Let's end today's study by writing declarations about God and why we can trust Him based on Psalm 46. For example: God is our fortress.

God is ________________________________.

God is ________________________________.

God is ________________________________.

God is ________________________________.

PRAYER PRACTICE

Return to Psalm 46 and read it aloud in first person as a personal declaration. Speak a prayer of adoration to God through the psalm.

Then, answer these questions about what you just declared:

Why do you believe this declaration psalm?

What evidence do you have to support your belief?

Submit your responses as an offering to the Lord.

1 Come, let us sing for joy to the LORD;
let us shout aloud to the Rock of our salvation.
2 Let us come before him with thanksgiving
and extol him with music and song.
3 For the LORD is the great God,
the great King above all gods.
4 In his hand are the depths of the earth,
and the mountain peaks belong to him.
5 The sea is his, for he made it,
and his hands formed the dry land.
6 Come, let us bow down in worship,
let us kneel before the LORD our Maker;
7 for he is our God
and we are the people of his pasture,
the flock under his care.
Today, if only you would hear his voice,
8 "Do not harden your hearts as you did at Meribah,
as you did that day at Massah in the wilderness,
9 where your ancestors tested me;
they tried me, though they had seen what I did.
10 For forty years I was angry with that generation;
I said, 'They are a people whose hearts go astray,
and they have not known my ways.'
11 So I declared on oath in my anger,
'They shall never enter my rest.'"

DAY 4

A Surrendered Praise

For the woman who struggles to find joy in her circumstances.

GLYNNIS WHITWER AND JACKIE SMITH-BELL

TODAY'S READING: Psalm 95

MAJOR MOMENT: God's people are called to approach Him with joyful hearts.

KEY VERSE: Psalm 95:1
Come, let us sing for joy to the LORD;
let us shout aloud to the Rock of our salvation.

Have you ever attended a concert or sporting event where the crowd roared with joy at the performance? People jump to their feet with shouts of approval. How exciting it is to celebrate the talent, excellence, hard work and success of someone we adore. It becomes transcendent, even, as for a moment all cares slip from thought.

How much more joyful should our celebration be in the presence of our heavenly Father, whose majesty and excellence are unmarred by the human frailty or inconsistency of those we follow on the stage or field?

Today we'll see that the psalmist who wrote Psalm 95 knew the importance of approaching the Lord in prayerful worship and always honoring Him. Even when our senses are startled, returning to what we know to be true about God's character restores our joy. He is our Comforter and our Rock (Deuteronomy 32:4) that remains steadfast and perfect in life's unsteady moments.

Psalm 95 has two distinct parts. The first is an exuberant invitation to come into the presence of God. The second is a distinct warning.

> Read Psalm 95:1-6 and list the activities we are called to participate in when we enter God's presence.

This approach to worship isn't subdued and spiritless. In fact, though it might feel a bit uncomfortable or maybe irreverent to *"sing for joy"* (v. 1), the psalmist set aside any thoughts of himself or his circumstances to celebrate the One he served.

We see a similar abandon when King David celebrated the return of the Ark of the Covenant in 2 Samuel 6. David's joy was uncontainable as he danced before the people.

Read 2 Samuel 6:16-22. What reason did David give for his celebration in verse 21? Can you identify similar reasons for you to rejoice in prayer?

It can be hard to praise God when our circumstances don't feel joyful. Yet we are called throughout Scripture to exercise and practice joy. Philippians 4:4 is one well-known verse, where Paul exhorts us to *"rejoice in the Lord always."*

List the reasons we can rejoice at all times, according to Psalm 95. How can focusing on God's attributes help us find true joy in His presence?

Starting at verse 8, the celebration shifts to warning. While this may seem odd, it might help us to remember the psalms were created for public worship. Scholars believe Psalm 95 might have been prepared for the Feast of Tabernacles, "when God's people re-lived, in token, their time of encampment in the wilderness."[1]

Psalm 95:8-10 reminds us of a time when Israel defied God and brought painful judgment on themselves (Numbers 14). However, the psalmist also reminds us that *"today, if only [we] would hear his voice,"* we can make a better choice: a choice to worship (Psalm 95:7). We can humble our hearts to pray and sing praises to God no matter our circumstance because He is the King of kings and Lord of lords. He has no rival. In His power, He holds the earth in His hands (Psalm 95:4).

Although the people had seen God's powerful miracles, they still doubted and questioned God. For example, the psalmist mentions Meribah, where the Israelites grumbled. (Numbers 20:2-13) The Hebrews' wanderings could be summed up in one word: unbelief. This unbelief displeased God, and He refused entrance into the promised land to the first generation of Israelites He delivered from Egypt. (Numbers 14)

God welcomes our honest questions in prayer. But there is a type of questioning that offends God.

What warning can we gain from Psalm 95:8-11 about the wrong way to question God?

How does cultivating praise in our prayers help keep our hearts right?

Psalm 95 tells us that even though God's people witnessed His power, they still doubted what He would do during their days of difficulty. Because of their inability to offer God uninhibited praise from hearts that trusted Him, God had told a disobedient generation of Israelites they would not enter His rest (Psalm 95:11). For this reason, the psalmist called God's people in the present to demonstrate a posture of prayer, bowing before a King who's worthy of all honor and praise (Psalm 95:6).

Years later, the writer of Hebrews also referred to Psalm 95 to urge Christians to rest in our praiseworthy Lord and cease from empty striving (Hebrews 4:1-7).

What's distracting you from wholeheartedly praising God in this season?

How can you practically surrender to Him today?

At the center of it all is Jesus. With Him in mind, we can respond to the psalmist's invitation to sing unto the Lord and surrender our prayers of praise out of the overflow of our hearts (Psalm 95:1).

PRAYER PRACTICE

Take a few minutes to complete these statements and then read what you have written as a prayer to Lord:

Lord, I sing for joy because ______________________________.

I come with thanksgiving for______________________________.

You, Lord are the great God, the great King above all gods.

In Your hand are______________________________.

I bow down in worship because of______________________________.

If I hear Your voice today, ______________________________.

Help me to honor and praise You, Lord.

Let me enter Your rest. Amen.

DOES GOD NEED OUR PRAISE?

As we reflect on the importance of adoration and why we should heed David's urging to *"sing for joy to the LORD"* (Psalm 95:1), we might find ourselves wondering ...

Does God really need to hear me tell Him how amazing He is all the time?

The short answer is: No. In fact, if the Lord needed our praises to validate Him, He would not be the Lord. Our triune God — Father, Son and Spirit — is perfectly fulfilled and perfectly adored in and of Himself. He needs nothing; He has everything. (Acts 17:24-25)

So praising God is fundamentally different from other kinds of praise we might be familiar with. We praise our children, for example, to encourage them when they do well on a test they studied hard for; otherwise, they may feel their efforts are unimportant. But God is never in danger of insecurity. We can't add to His importance — we can only recognize the supreme importance He already possesses. (Revelation 4:8; Revelation 21:6)

In other words: We praise God simply because He is infinitely praiseworthy. God doesn't *need* our prayers of adoration, but He *deserves* and *desires* them.

When Scripture tells us *"true worshipers ... are the kind of worshipers the Father seeks"* (John 4:23), this doesn't mean God is recruiting cheerleaders. He is inviting us to rightly see and know Him as Lord, and when we do that, praise is the inevitable result! As we tell God how amazing He is, we also remind ourselves that we are amazingly loved by Him — so God is pleased to receive the adoration He is due, and we are blessed and fulfilled by adoring Him.

PSALM 40

For the director of music. Of David. A psalm.

1 I waited patiently for the LORD;
he turned to me and heard my cry.
2 He lifted me out of the slimy pit,
out of the mud and mire;
he set my feet on a rock
and gave me a firm place to stand.
3 He put a new song in my mouth,
a hymn of praise to our God.
Many will see and fear the LORD
and put their trust in him.
4 Blessed is the one
who trusts in the LORD,
who does not look to the proud,
to those who turn aside to false gods.
5 Many, LORD my God,
are the wonders you have done,
the things you planned for us.
None can compare with you;
were I to speak and tell of your deeds,
they would be too many to declare.
6 Sacrifice and offering you did not desire—
but my ears you have opened—
burnt offerings and sin offerings you did not re-
quire.
7 Then I said, "Here I am, I have come—
it is written about me in the scroll.
8 I desire to do your will, my God;
your law is within my heart."
9 I proclaim your saving acts in the great assembly;
I do not seal my lips, LORD,
as you know.
10 I do not hide your righteousness in my heart;
I speak of your faithfulness and your saving help.
I do not conceal your love and your faithfulness
from the great assembly.
11 Do not withhold your mercy from me, LORD;
may your love and faithfulness always protect me.
12 For troubles without number surround me;
my sins have overtaken me, and I cannot see.
They are more than the hairs of my head,
and my heart fails within me.
13 Be pleased to save me, LORD;
come quickly, LORD, to help me.
14 May all who want to take my life
be put to shame and confusion;
may all who desire my ruin
be turned back in disgrace.
15 May those who say to me, "Aha! Aha!"
be appalled at their own shame.
16 But may all who seek you
rejoice and be glad in you;
may those who long for your saving help always say,
"The LORD is great!"
17 But as for me, I am poor and needy;
may the Lord think of me.
You are my help and my deliverer;
you are my God, do not delay.

DAY 5

While You Wait

For the woman who needs a revelation of who God really is.

GLYNNIS WHITWER AND KATY MCCOWN

TODAY'S READING: Psalm 40

MAJOR MOMENT: David praised God as his Deliverer and asked to be rescued again.

KEY VERSE: Psalm 40:3

He put a new song in my mouth,
a hymn of praise to our God.
Many will see and fear the LORD
and put their trust in him.

We close our week together by looking at Psalm 40, which is often considered a thanksgiving psalm and was written by King David. In addition to thanksgiving, we also see elements of praise and petition. Even though this isn't designated as a "psalm of adoration" by theologians, every part of the Bible, including Psalm 40, reveals who God is.

The first verses of Psalm 40 record a moment of celebration when David praised God for taking care of him in a terrifying situation. The two psalms prior to Psalm 40 detail David's pleas for God to answer him and express David's resolve to wait for Him (Psalm 38:15; Psalm 39:7). Psalm 40 confirms God leaned down and heard David's cry for help (Psalm 40:1), and this psalm seems to be written from a place of deliverance and prosperity.

It's not until we arrive at the closing verses that we find David wrote these words from a place of need yet again (Psalm 40:12-17). He described himself as *"poor and needy"* (Psalm 40:17) and desperate for deliverance. One scholar, Gerald Wilson, notes that the wording used in Psalm 40:12 denotes immediate, life-threatening circumstances as well as being on the brink of losing all hope.

Yet in the midst of his desperation, as David waited on God to deliver him again, he chose to pray and remember the truth of who God is. Recalling what God had done for him in the past gave David hope for what God would do for him in the future.

Our exercise today is to read through Psalm 40 and underline or highlight words or phrases that tell us something about God's character. Then, to the right of the psalm, identify the characteristics of God and note why He is worthy of praise. (We've completed verse 1 for you as an example below.)

As you make your list, you'll find so many reasons to praise God for who He is to you.

PSALM 40

For the director of music. Of David. A psalm.

1 I waited patiently for the LORD;
he turned to me and heard my cry.
2 He lifted me out of the slimy pit,
out of the mud and mire;
he set my feet on a rock
and gave me a firm place to stand.
3 He put a new song in my mouth,
a hymn of praise to our God.
Many will see and fear the LORD
and put their trust in him.
4 Blessed is the one
who trusts in the LORD,
who does not look to the proud,
to those who turn aside to false gods.
5 Many, LORD my God,
are the wonders you have done,
the things you planned for us.
None can compare with you;
were I to speak and tell of your deeds,
they would be too many to declare.
6 Sacrifice and offering you did not desire—
but my ears you have opened—
burnt offerings and sin offerings you did not require.

NOTES

V. 1 — God listens to His children and draws near to us. He isn't aloof but is compassionate and caring.

NOTES

7 Then I said, "Here I am, I have come—
it is written about me in the scroll.
8 I desire to do your will, my God;
your law is within my heart."
9 I proclaim your saving acts in the great assembly;
I do not seal my lips, LORD,
as you know.
10 I do not hide your righteousness in my heart;
I speak of your faithfulness and your saving help.
I do not conceal your love and your faithfulness
from the great assembly.
11 Do not withhold your mercy from me, LORD;
may your love and faithfulness always protect me.
12 For troubles without number surround me;
my sins have overtaken me, and I cannot see.
They are more than the hairs of my head,
and my heart fails within me.
13 Be pleased to save me, LORD;
come quickly, LORD, to help me.
14 May all who want to take my life
be put to shame and confusion;
may all who desire my ruin
be turned back in disgrace.
15 May those who say to me, "Aha! Aha!"
be appalled at their own shame.
16 But may all who seek you
rejoice and be glad in you;
may those who long for your saving help always say,
"The LORD is great!"
17 But as for me, I am poor and needy;
may the Lord think of me.
You are my help and my deliverer;
you are my God, do not delay.

NOTE FROM JOEL

In this psalm, we see the character of God, and the action of God is consistent with His character. First, there is a petition from the psalmist: In verse 1, there is a cry from the child of God. But then notice God's **three actions** after He hears the cry of His child:

1. He draws us up.

2. He sets our feet.

3. He puts a new song in our mouth.

These actions of God provide **three comforts** for us:

1. We are brought high, a phrase that speaks of honor bestowed upon us.

2. He grants us the stability we long for. When things are out of control, we find stability in the One who holds all things together.

3. We sing because we've experienced the goodness of God.

And just as David chose to dwell on God's character, we, too, can pray to our Lord in joyful adoration of who He is. King David's words resonate with the later instructions of the Apostle Paul to the Christians in Philippi:

- *"Rejoice in the Lord always"* (Philippians 4:4).
- *"Do not be anxious about anything, but in every situation, by prayer and petition, with thanksgiving, present your requests to God"* (Philippians 4:6).
- *"If anything is excellent or praiseworthy—think about such things"* (Philippians 4:8).

God is the only One who is truly excellent and praiseworthy. We can be sure He is always a safe place for our thoughts to dwell. And with David's example and Paul's instructions in mind, we can celebrate God's wondrous works even while we wait for God to answer our pleas. We can think on His righteousness, steadfast love, justice and faithfulness ... but we don't have to stop at thinking about God with our minds; through prayer, we can also speak to Him from our hearts.

REFLECTION QUESTIONS

David begins this psalm by remembering God's faithfulness. What happens in our relationship with God when we do the same?

David is honest about his failures and vulnerable enough to share them with others. What must David have believed about God to move him to such honesty?

In the next few days, who is one person you could tell about God's faithfulness to you?

PRAYER PRACTICE

To complete the week, simply reflect on what you know of the Lord our God, His character, His will, His love, care and promise. Write a prayer of adoration and rest in the holy communion and conversation with our Lord.

WEEKEND REFLECTION

As we come to the end of our first week of this study, it's good to remind ourselves why we started a study of prayer and psalms with the concept of adoration or praise. To answer that question, let's move to the New Testament book of Matthew, where religious leaders asked Jesus a question: *"Teacher, which is the greatest commandment in the Law?"* (Matthew 22:36).

Jesus' answer helps us understand why it's important to cultivate praise into our prayers: *"'Love the Lord your God with all your heart and with all your soul and with all your mind.' This is the first and greatest commandment"* (Matthew 22:37-38).

Prayers of adoration help us grow in our love and affection for God — not just for what He can do for us but for who He is. If we wanted to show intentional love to a friend or a family member, we probably wouldn't first present a list of requests or ask their forgiveness. Those things might happen, but we'd start with a declaration of love, possibly including specific examples of what we love about them.

The same idea can be applied to God but in greater measure.

One day, every creature on earth and in heaven will praise God. Every knee will bow in reverence to Him. Creating a habit of praise in your prayers will open your eyes to what heaven already knows: He is worthy!

Then I heard every creature in heaven and on earth and under the earth and on the sea, and all that is in them, saying: "To him who sits on the throne and to the Lamb be praise and honor and glory and power, for ever and ever!" (Revelation 5:13)

A PRAYER FOR YOU

Great are You, Lord! You are my help and my deliverer. You hear Your children's prayers, and You know when we are in despair. I praise You for Your perfect compassion that moves You to act for my good. Your goodness has never failed; You've never abandoned a promise. I'm so grateful that You think of me and love me. In Jesus' name, amen.

WEEK TWO

PRAYERS OF CONFESSION

Of David.

[1] In you, LORD my God,
  I put my trust.
[2] I trust in you;
  do not let me be put to shame,
  nor let my enemies triumph over me.
[3] No one who hopes in you
  will ever be put to shame,
but shame will come on those
  who are treacherous without cause.
[4] Show me your ways, LORD,
  teach me your paths.
[5] Guide me in your truth and teach me,
  for you are God my Savior,
  and my hope is in you all day long.
[6] Remember, LORD, your great mercy and love,
  for they are from of old.
[7] Do not remember the sins of my youth
  and my rebellious ways;
according to your love remember me,
  for you, LORD, are good.
[8] Good and upright is the LORD;
  therefore he instructs sinners in his ways.
[9] He guides the humble in what is right
  and teaches them his way.
[10] All the ways of the LORD are loving and faithful
  toward those who keep the demands of his covenant.
[11] For the sake of your name, LORD,
  forgive my iniquity, though it is great.
[12] Who, then, are those who fear the LORD?
  He will instruct them in the ways they should choose.
[13] They will spend their days in prosperity,
  and their descendants will inherit the land.
[14] The LORD confides in those who fear him;
  he makes his covenant known to them.
[15] My eyes are ever on the LORD,
  for only he will release my feet from the snare.
[16] Turn to me and be gracious to me,
  for I am lonely and afflicted.
[17] Relieve the troubles of my heart
  and free me from my anguish.
[18] Look on my affliction and my distress
  and take away all my sins.
[19] See how numerous are my enemies
  and how fiercely they hate me!
[20] Guard my life and rescue me;
  do not let me be put to shame,
  for I take refuge in you.
[21] May integrity and uprightness protect me,
  because my hope, LORD, is in you.
[22] Deliver Israel, O God,
  from all their troubles!

DAY 6

For His Name's Sake

For the woman who desperately wants to change.

MEGHAN RYAN AND BETHANY RUTH

TODAY'S READING: Psalm 25

MAJOR MOMENT: David brought his sins before God and asked Him for instruction on how to live.

KEY VERSE: Psalm 25:11
For the sake of your name, LORD, forgive my iniquity, though it is great.

We aren't exactly born with a desire to admit our mistakes. If you've ever spent time with toddlers, you know they don't willingly admit when they have been disobedient. We are born with a bent to sin and to cover it up when we do.

Can we ever change?

This week, we will shift our focus to prayers of confession. Now, before you close this book and walk away because that sounds too hard, let's get a different perspective. By definition, confession is an act of faith.

> First John 1:9 says we confess our sins because God *"is faithful and just and will forgive us our sins and purify us from all unrighteousness."* And a profession of faith is also a kind of confession: Romans 10:9 says, *"If you declare with your mouth, 'Jesus is Lord,' and believe in your heart that God raised him from the dead, you will be saved."*

What is your current understanding of confession?

How does it make you feel?

The Hebrew word most often translated as "confess" in Scripture is *yādâh,* but this complex word contains more than just the idea of saying "I'm sorry." *Yādâh* carries the idea of acknowledging our sin *and* praising God for who He is. When true worshippers approach God in prayerful confession, our hearts demonstrate repentance, a genuine change, and we can walk in restored relationship with Him.

Let's study a beautiful psalm of confession by David today and use it to guide our understanding of how we too can confess in prayer and humility. How God desires to hear our confession and how trustworthy He is with it!

David brought his sins before God. While we don't know the circumstances he faced, we do know that in asking God to save him, he admitted he was not innocent.

> How many times does David use the words *"sin," "transgression," "guilt," "trouble," "afflict"* or *"shame"* in the English Standard Version of Psalm 25?

While the word *yādâh* is not in Psalm 25, David displays confession throughout this psalm.

This psalm was written in a literary form called a "chiasm." Often used in ancient Hebrew writing, chiastic structure presents a series of ideas, then offers the same or similar ideas again in reverse order. So, the pattern of Psalm 25 would look something like this if we could see it visually: **A B C D E D C B A.**

Return to the psalm and see if you can label the verses according to the chiasm.

David's confession of his sins didn't leave him in despair and dismay; it reminded him of his desperate need for God. He knew God was the only One who could rescue him.

Notice the elements A, B, C and D are doubled, but the central idea E is unique and often the most important idea. The main idea of this psalm would be found in verse 11: *"For the sake of your name, Lord, forgive my iniquity, though it is great."*

To see how David built up to verse 11, let's look back at how he began this prayer: with a cry to the Lord. His circumstances prompted him to lift up his soul and wait for God to accept his expression of dependence (Psalm 25:1-3). This opening cry stands in parallel to David's final expression of dependence, waiting again for God's action on his behalf, pleading for God to guard his very life (Psalm 25:20-22).

We find another parallel in David's corresponding prayers for guidance: first that God would lead and guide him *into* Truth (Psalm 25:4-5), then that God would lead him *out of* trouble and distress (Psalm 25:17-19).

THE CHIASTIC STRUCTURE OF PSALM 25

A VERSES 1-3

B VERSES 4-5

C VERSES 6-7

D VERSES 8-10

E VERSE 11

D VERSES 12-14

C VERSES 15-16

B VERSES 17-19

A VERSES 20-22

David wanted to walk in God's paths, and he realized only God could teach him how. David knew the God of his salvation would restore him from sin and lead him in His right ways.

David also offered two corresponding praises, once in Psalm 25:6-7 and again in Psalm 25:15-16, as he reflected on God's mercy and steadfast love. David knew God's forgiveness is based on His character, so he turned his eyes toward God and asked God to turn toward him.

Finally, David's praise moved him to reflect on God's covenant, or His promises to His people (Psalm 25:8-10). David knew when he approached God in humble confession, God would maintain His faithful covenant love. Then after his confession in verse 11, David viewed the covenant from the perspective of one humbled and forgiven, one who feared the Lord and received the benefits of His promises (Psalm 25:12-14).

At the center of David's psalm is the wonderful truth that God's forgiveness is always His gracious response when we humbly confess to Him in prayer. He forgives because His actions always reflect who He is. God's *name* reflects God's *character,* and even great guilt is forgiven because of our great God (Psalm 25:11).

David does three things in his confession that we can also practice:

1. Reference God's character. Throughout this psalm, David stated characteristics of God. His love is steadfast, (v. 10) He is good, (v. 8) He does not put us to shame, (v. 3) and He pardons our guilt. (v. 11)

> What other characteristics of God does David mention in his prayer? Write some here, and highlight some in your Bible too.

2. Remember what He has done. Knowing that God instructed and brought His people out of their distress in the past (*"from of old"*) gives us hope that we, too, can move forward after we sin (vv. 6-7).

3. Remind ourselves of what God *will* do because of who He is. In referencing God's characteristics, David reminded himself that God would forgive him, instruct him and deliver him from trouble. (vv. 3, 8, 15)

Friend, change is possible. Confession is the first step toward humility and admitting that we can't do anything on our own apart from God.

How have you sought communion and closeness with God through prayers of confession when you found yourself, like David, in the net of sin?

What patterns or behaviors in your life feel impossible to overcome?

What does Luke 1:37 say about what is impossible for God?

Confession is not about feeling shame. Confession is freedom from the *weight of shame.* **When we stop hiding, we start healing.**

Read Romans 8:1 and fill in the blanks: *"Therefore, there is now no* ______________________ *for those who are in* ____________ __________*."*

PRAYER PRACTICE

To end our day of studying Psalm 25, write a chiastic prayer, like David did, for the Lord to teach you His path (v. 4) as you practice confession today. Try a simple pattern like this:

A

B

C

B

A

PSALM 32

Of David. A *maskil.*

1 Blessed is the one
whose transgressions are forgiven,
whose sins are covered.
2 Blessed is the one
whose sin the LORD does not count against them
and in whose spirit is no deceit.
3 When I kept silent,
my bones wasted away
through my groaning all day long.
4 For day and night
your hand was heavy on me;
my strength was sapped
as in the heat of summer.
5 Then I acknowledged my sin to you
and did not cover up my iniquity.
I said, "I will confess
my transgressions to the LORD."
And you forgave
the guilt of my sin.

6 Therefore let all the faithful pray to you
while you may be found;
surely the rising of the mighty waters
will not reach them.
7 You are my hiding place;
you will protect me from trouble
and surround me with songs of deliverance.
8 I will instruct you and teach you in the way you should go;
I will counsel you with my loving eye on you.
9 Do not be like the horse or the mule,
which have no understanding
but must be controlled by bit and bridle
or they will not come to you.
10 Many are the woes of the wicked,
but the LORD's unfailing love
surrounds the one who trusts in him.
11 Rejoice in the LORD and be glad, you righteous;
sing, all you who are upright in heart!

DAY 7

(Honest) Communication Is Key

For the woman who wants to be freed from the weight of what she's done.

MEGHAN RYAN AND SANDELL SNYDER

TODAY'S READING: Psalm 32

MAJOR MOMENT: Those who are forgiven by God are blessed by Him.

KEY VERSE: Psalm 32:3
When I kept silent, my bones wasted away through my groaning all day long.

One of the most beautiful parts of confession is getting to experience forgiveness. Whether we receive forgiveness from another person or especially from God, there is a joy that comes from being forgiven. Psalm 32 offers us the ultimate application of this life-giving truth: Prayers of confession are honest conversations with God that open our hearts to the gift, and the *Giver,* of forgiveness.

> Read Isaiah 1:18 and Micah 7:19. How does it make you feel to know the result of confession is God's forgiveness?

When we are in Christ, nothing we do can outweigh His love for us. Over and over again, He is faithful and just to forgive us when we sin. This is good news!

In today's psalm, there are four Hebrew terms used for "sin." Circle the word "sin" throughout the psalm.

MULTIPLE WORDS ARE USED FOR "SIN" IN THIS PSALM, HIGHLIGHTING DIFFERENT ASPECTS OF SIN:

Aspects of Sin

"transgression" (vv. 1, 5) *pesha'*	denotes the basic idea of rebellion.
"sin" (v. 1) *hata'ah*	a more general term referring to a deliberate offense.
"iniquity"" (v. 5) *awon*	implies crime and going astray.
"deceit" (v. 2) *remiyyah*	emphasizes falsehood or even hypocrisy.

THERE ARE ALSO THREE DIFFERENT HEBREW PHRASES IN PSALM 32 THAT COMMUNICATE THE STATE OF THE ONE WHOSE SIN IS FORGIVEN.

Aspects of Forgiveness

pesha' nsuy'	"transgression forgiven"	to be unburdened
hata'ah ksuy'	"sin covered"	to have an offense covered
yahsob' lo awon	"iniquity does not count against them"	to be legally acquitted

Which of these aspects of sin do you think is easiest for you to recognize in yourself? Why?

Which one is easier to miss? Why?

Reread Psalm 32:6-7. What happens when we offer prayers of confession?

What did David say God was for him?

When we confess in prayer, not only do we **find God,** but He also **hides us** from the eternal consequences of our sin. We may read about the joy of the *"upright"* (v. 11) and feel unworthy of this — but when Jesus rose from the grave, He made a way for us to receive His uprightness. That means in Christ, we are lifted out of our sin. We are covered. We aren't liable for punishment. It's not confession that saves us. It's Jesus who saves us. (John 1:29)

David described his personal experience with confessional prayer when he wrote Psalm 32, teaching God's people the immeasurable value of confession. The precise translation of the psalm's original Hebrew title, "A *maskil,*" is unclear, but its roots suggest that it is a poem of contemplation, likely meant for instruction.

In this psalm, David humbly acknowledged the depth and breadth of his own failings to show us that confession applies to the full spectrum of sin — *"transgression," "sin," "iniquity"* and *"deceit"*— and makes way for complete forgiveness (ESV). No type of offense is excluded!

He then used the three mirror opposites of those terms to express the all-encompassing nature of God's forgiveness: He lifts the burden of our sin, covers us with His grace (Psalm 32:5), and clears our record of wrongdoing (Psalm 32:2). It no longer counts against us. God's forgiveness releases us from all the ways sin enslaves us.

David knew confession makes a pathway to joy, security and love, but notice that he learned these things the hard way: *"When I kept silent, my bones wasted away ... "* (Psalm 32:3). Or as the New Living Translation states, *"When I refused to confess ..."* (Psalm 32:3). For a time, David stubbornly refused to engage honestly with God about his sin. How common it is for us, too, to ignore or hide our rebellions and mistakes. Sometimes our pride suggests we can handle them on our own, or sometimes shame makes our sins seem too painful to mention. Either way, our sin is compounded by denial.

It is actually God's mercy that allows us to experience the pain our sin and silence cause as they separate us from Him. David described feeling God's *"heavy"* hand of discipline or displeasure (Psalm 32:4), but that pressure ultimately moved David to end his silence. His prayers of confession signified his return to God and prepared his heart for the blessings of reconciliation.

When David stopped hiding *from* God, he found that he could be hidden *in* God instead (Psalm 32:7). No matter how overwhelming our sin may feel, we will find the same thing when we open our mouths in honest prayers of confession.

The problem is that because we are sinful, we don't want to admit we sin! But thankfully, God gave us the Holy Spirit, who convicts us. (John 16:8) Only by His power do we experience heart change.

What happens to us when we unwisely avoid confession?

What situations do you find the most difficult to talk honestly with God about?

How can God's promise of forgiveness help you overcome the fear/pride/shame that holds you back from open communication?

At its core, confession is about repentance. Confession requires that we acknowledge we have gone astray and need God's intervention to be saved. Repentance requires that we willingly change direction and return to Him.

Jesus beautifully illustrated this very concept, and how the Father responds to those who return to Him, in the parable of the prodigal son (Luke 15:11-24). The younger son in this parable made a series of unwise and disrespectful decisions that led him far away from his father and his home. When the consequences of his decisions started to bear down upon him, he could no longer deny his mistakes. He made the decision to return and be honest about what he had done. He knew he didn't deserve reconciliation as a son; he hoped only for a place among his father's servants. And yet, *"while he was still a long way off, his father saw him and was filled with compassion for him; he ran to his son, threw his arms around him and kissed him"* (Luke 15:20b). The humbleness of heart that led him home opened wide the door to forgiveness and the loving embrace of the father.

The forgiven are blessed!

PRAYER PRACTICE

Let's practice confession by praying like David in Psalm 32.

Father, Your Word says the one whose transgression is forgiven and whose sin is covered is blessed. (Psalm 31:1) Let there be no iniquity or deceit in me. (v. 2) When I am silent in my sin, I waste away. But when I acknowledge it and don't cover it up, You forgive me. (vv. 3–5) So I confess my sins before You now and turn away from them. Thank You for being my hiding place, preserving me from my trouble, and surrounding me with shouts of deliverance. (v. 7) Teach me. Counsel me. Surround me with Your steadfast love because I trust in You. I will be glad and shout for joy! (vv. 9–11) In Jesus' name, amen.

A psalm of David. A petition.

1 LORD, do not rebuke me in your anger
or discipline me in your wrath.
2 Your arrows have pierced me,
and your hand has come down on me.
3 Because of your wrath there is no health
in my body;
there is no soundness in my bones be-
cause of my sin.
4 My guilt has overwhelmed me
like a burden too heavy to bear.
5 My wounds fester and are loathsome
because of my sinful folly.
6 I am bowed down and brought very low;
all day long I go about mourning.
7 My back is filled with searing pain;
there is no health in my body.
8 I am feeble and utterly crushed;
I groan in anguish of heart.
9 All my longings lie open before you, Lord;
my sighing is not hidden from you.
10 My heart pounds, my strength fails me;
even the light has gone from my eyes.
11 My friends and companions avoid me be-
cause of my wounds;
my neighbors stay far away.
12 Those who want to kill me set their traps,
those who would harm me talk of my ruin;
all day long they scheme and lie.
13 I am like the deaf, who cannot hear,
like the mute, who cannot speak;
14 I have become like one who does not hear,
whose mouth can offer no reply.
15 LORD, I wait for you;
you will answer, Lord my God.
16 For I said, "Do not let them gloat
or exalt themselves over me when my feet
slip."
17 For I am about to fall,
and my pain is ever with me.
18 I confess my iniquity;
I am troubled by my sin.
19 Many have become my enemies without
cause;
those who hate me without reason are
numerous.
20 Those who repay my good with evil
lodge accusations against me,
though I seek only to do what is good.
21 LORD, do not forsake me;
do not be far from me, my God.
22 Come quickly to help me,
my Lord and my Savior.

DAY 8

Consequences and Confession

For the woman who feels like something is blocking her from God.

MEGHAN RYAN AND SANDY JOHNSON

TODAY'S READING: Psalm 38

MAJOR MOMENT: David honestly asked God for forgiveness to draw near to Him.

KEY VERSES: Psalm 38:17-1

For I am about to fall, and my pain is ever with me. I confess my iniquity; I am troubled by my sin.

When we mess up, it can feel hard to come to God. Whether it's because we feel ashamed or because we don't know how to fix what's been done, approaching God after we have sinned can be the last thing we want to do. But the reality is: Confessing is the best thing we can do so nothing is standing between us and God.

> Describe a moment in your life when you felt like something was blocking you from God. What was the blockage?

Psalm 38 is subtitled "a petition." Some translations may say "to bring remembrance" (CSB) or "for the memorial offering" (ESV). Throughout Scripture, requesting that God remember something was another way of asking Him to act in a situation.[1]

> Take a few minutes to write down some words and phrases David used to describe how he felt in this prayer. What did he want God to do?

In addition to being a psalm of confession, this is also a psalm of lament, a type of prayer that draws us closer to God when we are suffering or in pain (which we will talk more about in a couple weeks). Lament is appropriate for prayers of confession because our sin should grieve us. (2 Corinthians 7:10)

Sin separates us from God unless and until we repent. (Isaiah 59:1-2) It hurts us. It hurts others. What breaks God's heart should break our hearts too.

Have you ever thought about grieving your sin? What do you think that would look like?

Take a few moments to examine your heart and life. Are there places where you are intentionally, or even unintentionally, distant from God?

Although there is no specific mention of what sin was plaguing David in this chapter, he was clearly suffering physical, emotional and social consequences of his own sinful choices:

Physically, David was apparently afflicted with a painful disease. He described his pain as that of being pierced with arrows (Psalm 38:2), having *"no health in [his] body"* (Psalm 38:3), having *"wounds [that] fester"* (Psalm 38:5), and being *"filled with searing pain"* (Psalm 38:7).

Emotionally, David felt weighed down by the burden of his sin (Psalm 38:4). The guilt and shame caused him to feel crushed in spirit (Psalm 38:8).

Socially, David also felt isolated, deserted by those he loved: *"My friends and companions avoid me because of my wounds; my neighbors stay far away"* (Psalm 38:11). At his weakest and loneliest, he found himself the target of his enemies' plans to harm him (Psalm 38:12).

David recognized that all these pain points were ultimately connected to his sin. So when David cried out to God, he didn't hide his sin or blame others for it but rather acknowledged his *"folly"* (Psalm 38:5). And as we read in our key verses today, he confessed and was sorry (Psalms 38:17-18).

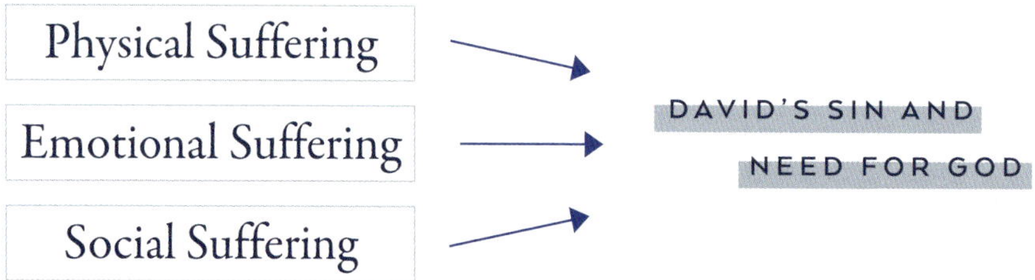

In "real time" in Psalm 38, we see David realize that God didn't separate Himself from David; David separated himself from God. But the good news is that God's kindness leads us to repentance. (Romans 2:4) He wants to remove anything that separates us from Him. That's why He sent Jesus. Jesus lived the sinless life we couldn't and died to make a way for our sins to be forgiven.

> When you think about God's kindness leading us to repentance, does it make you want to be honest with Him about your mistakes and sins? Why or why not?

Psalm 38:9 gives us hope to cling to: *"All my longings lie open before you, Lord; my sighing is not hidden from you."*

As he suffered from the physical, emotional and social effects of his own sin, David's heartfelt cries to God were unfiltered and raw. He didn't blame God or make excuses but rather asked God to help him and not forsake him (Psalm 38:21-22). You too can go to God honestly in prayer and receive the mercy and forgiveness only He can offer.

PRAYER PRACTICE

When we're grieving our own sin like David was in Psalm 38, feeling sorrow about the circumstances in our lives and the world around us, we can follow these four steps of prayer, found in most examples of biblical confession, and bring our pain to God:

1. Turn to God rather than ignore the pain (Psalm 4:1; Psalm 130:1).

"All my longings lie open before you, Lord; my sighing is not hidden from you" (Psalm 38:9).

2. Tell God your complaint and confession (Psalm 6:6-7; Psalm 39:11).

"My heart pounds, my strength fails me; even the light has gone from my eyes. My friends and companions avoid me because of my wounds; my neighbors stay far away" (Psalm 38:10-11).

3. Ask God for what you want from Him (Psalm 17:13-14; Psalm 43:1).

"Lord, do not forsake me; do not be far from me, my God. Come quickly to help me, my Lord and my Savior" (Psalm 38:21-22).

4. Trust God and His promises (Psalm 13:5-6; Psalm 31:14).

"Lord, I wait for you; you will answer, Lord my God" (Psalm 38:15).

For the director of music. A psalm of David. When the prophet Nathan came to him after David had committed adultery with Bathsheba.

1 Have mercy on me, O God,
according to your unfailing love;
according to your great compassion
blot out my transgressions.
2 Wash away all my iniquity
and cleanse me from my sin.
3 For I know my transgressions,
and my sin is always before me.
4 Against you, you only, have I sinned
and done what is evil in your sight;
so you are right in your verdict
and justified when you judge.
5 Surely I was sinful at birth,
sinful from the time my mother conceived me.
6 Yet you desired faithfulness even in the womb;
you taught me wisdom in that secret place.
7 Cleanse me with hyssop, and I will be clean;
wash me, and I will be whiter than snow.
8 Let me hear joy and gladness;
let the bones you have crushed rejoice.
9 Hide your face from my sins
and blot out all my iniquity.
10 Create in me a pure heart, O God,
and renew a steadfast spirit within me.
11 Do not cast me from your presence
or take your Holy Spirit from me.
12 Restore to me the joy of your salvation
and grant me a willing spirit, to sustain me.
13 Then I will teach transgressors your ways,
so that sinners will turn back to you.
14 Deliver me from the guilt of bloodshed,
O God,
you who are God my Savior,
and my tongue will sing of your righteousness.
15 Open my lips, Lord,
and my mouth will declare your praise.
16 You do not delight in sacrifice, or I would
bring it;
you do not take pleasure in burnt offerings.
17 My sacrifice, O God, is a broken spirit;
a broken and contrite heart
you, God, will not despise.
18 May it please you to prosper Zion,
to build up the walls of Jerusalem.
19 Then you will delight in the sacrifices of the
righteous,
in burnt offerings offered whole;
then bulls will be offered on your altar.

DAY 9

The Power of Confession

For the woman who is tired of hiding.

MEGHAN RYAN

TODAY'S READING: Psalm 51

MAJOR MOMENT: David confessed his sins to God and did not try to hide them.

KEY VERSE: Psalm 51:1
*Have mercy on me, O God, according to your unfailing love;
according to your great compassion blot out my transgressions.*

David was known as a man after God's own heart. (1 Samuel 13:14) But David wrote today's psalm after the prophet Nathan confronted him for a very big problem he caused by committing a series of sins. David slept with a married woman and then killed her husband to cover it up (see 2 Samuel 11-12). Not exactly the poster child for following after God ...

Read 2 Samuel 12:13. What was David's response to Nathan?

Nathan's willingness to speak truth softened David's heart to repent before God. Instead of letting his offense or anger get in the way, he went straight to God to ask for forgiveness, cleansing and restoration.

How would you feel if you had a friend call out something you did wrong? Would you be angry or receptive? Do you have friends in your life who hold you accountable to God's Word?

David confessed. He stopped hiding. He did not blame anyone else. In Psalm 51, he asked God to *"blot out [his] transgressions"* (v. 1), *"cleanse"* him (v. 2) and *"deliver"* him from his guilt and sin (v. 14).

NOTE FROM JOEL

The Hebrew word David uses to describe God's love translated as "faithful love" is ***hesed,*** and it is rich with meaning.

(ḥĕ·sĕḏ): n.masc.; ≡ Str 2617; **loyal love,** unfailing kindness, devotion, i.e., a love or affection that is steadfast based on a prior relationship

Let's reread Psalm 51:10-12. What three things did David ask God?

1. "____________ *in me a pure heart, O God, and renew a steadfast spirit within me."* (v. 10)
2. "_____ _____ _______ *me from your presence or take your Holy Spirit from me."* (v. 11)
3. "___________ *to me the joy of your salvation and grant me a willing spirit, to sustain me."* (v. 12)

None of these things could David do on his own. He needed God to do a work within him. In his confession, he allowed God to renew and restore him.

And God answered David's prayer. We know this because for the rest of his life, David sought the Lord, and the Lord continued to forgive him when he made mistakes again (e.g., 2 Samuel 24). What David did was sin, and it had consequences, but it **still** wasn't too much for God to forgive and redeem.

The same is true for you and me. Whatever mistake we feel too afraid to say out loud, the thing we fear someone finding out about us, it's not too much for God.

If you are tired of hiding, come to Him. Tell a trusted friend, too, if you feel led. There is so much power in not having to hide. It reminds us that in Christ, we are free. And we can live like that is true.

Insight *on* Psalm 51

LYSA TERKEURST

As I was studying this passage, I saw through David's example what God wants us to do with the guilt we feel. God wants guilt to lead us to repentance. He does not want our guilt to be left unattended and turn into a shame that imprisons us. There's also a progression King David outlines for us that I want to highlight in our study today:

ONE

Confession

Psalm 51:1-6

Even though David's confession wasn't immediate, it is complete. He pours out his heart before the Lord, making no excuses or justifications for his sins. In verse 4 he says *"Against you, you only, have I sinned and done what is evil in your sight, so that you may be justified in your words and blameless in your judgment"* (ESV).

It can be intimidating to show up before God in complete honesty, but David models something so beautiful for us here. When we really understand the deep mercy and steadfast love of God, we will be less afraid to crack open our hearts and confess our sins to Him.

TWO

Cleansing

Psalm 51:7-9

In verse 7, there's a shift in David's words, revealing that confession has stopped and now the cleansing can begin. David uses words like *"purge", "clean",* and *"wash"* to describe this.

Cleansing isn't usually a fun process, but it is a necessary process. Even in a trivial example like laundry, cleansing causes separation between what is tainted and what is pure. And the same is true of our hearts. After confession, it is so crucial that we surrender ourselves to the process of cleansing so that the Lord can make us pure (Matthew 5:8).

THREE

Creation

Psalm 51:10-12

Next, David takes cleansing to a deeper level by asking God to *"create in me a clean heart"* (v. 10). The word "create" doesn't mean to take something old and make it better. No, this word means to take something from nothing and make it *brand new.* It's the same "create" from Genesis when God created out of nothing. If God creates a new heart in us, in a spiritual sense, our hearts will be less prone to return to what caused us to sin in the first place.

FOUR

Calling

Psalm 51:13-17

What the enemy meant to use this for — a whole lot of evil, disruption and heartbreak — God can take it and make it good. One way this is fulfilled is through our *calling.* At the very beginning of verse 13, David says, *"Then..."* and this transition is so important.

The word *then* reveals this process David had to go through to get here (confession, cleansing and creation). God wants to use our past sin choices to help other people — but in due time. There is great purpose to our pain. There is a great opportunity to help others walk through something difficult in a more God-honoring way even than we did. All of this is true. But also, David lays out a *progression* for us to walk through before we jump from the test to the testimony. God wants to make progress in our healing before we begin helping other people.

So, this progression shows us how to walk through each step so that we don't short-circuit any stage. This doesn't mean we wait to help others until we're perfect. We'll never be there. But we should apply wisdom and ask God to help us discern the timing of how he might use the experiences we've been through.

Friend, wherever you find yourself, remember King David's example: God wants us to come to Him with our guilt, not hide from Him in our guilt.

PRAYER PRACTICE

Rewrite Psalm 51:10–12 in your own words today. Offer them as a blessing and honor to the Lord.

A song of ascents.

1 Out of the depths I cry to you, LORD;
2 Lord, hear my voice.
Let your ears be attentive
  to my cry for mercy.
3 If you, LORD, kept a record of sins,
  Lord, who could stand?
4 But with you there is forgiveness,
  so that we can, with reverence, serve you.
5 I wait for the LORD, my whole being waits,
  and in his word I put my hope.
6 I wait for the Lord
  more than watchmen wait for the morning,
  more than watchmen wait for the morning.
7 Israel, put your hope in the LORD,
  for with the LORD is unfailing love
  and with him is full redemption.
8 He himself will redeem Israel
  from all their sins.

DAY 10

Mea Culpa

For the woman who wants to live free from fear and shame.

MEGHAN RYAN AND QUANTRILLA ARD

TODAY'S READING: Psalm 130

MAJOR MOMENT: David put his hope in God's forgiveness as he waited on the Lord.

KEY VERSE: Psalm 130:4

But with you there is forgiveness, so that we can, with reverence, serve you.

To wrap up our week, let's look at one last psalm: Psalm 130. Read the psalm below, along with the notes and questions we've included alongside it, and consider how it relates to what we've studied this week. Let's deeply dig into the text to discover all God wants to teach us about prayer through these words.

Feel free to add your own notes, underlining and highlighting as you read! Consider underlining the things God does or will do, and highlighting the things David does or will do. Then make some notes: Who is more active? Who gives, and who receives?

PSALM 130	NOTES
A song of ascents.	
1 Out of the depths I cry to you, LORD;	*Confession starts with admitting our need for God.*
2 Lord, hear my voice.	
Let your ears be attentive	
to my cry for mercy.	*God will hear David.*
3 If you, LORD, kept a record of sins,	
Lord, who could stand?	
4 But with you there is forgiveness,	
so that we can, with reverence, serve you.	*David begs for mercy as he confesses; he is powerless.*
5 I wait for the LORD, my whole being waits,	

and in his word I put my hope.
6 I wait for the Lord
more than watchmen wait for the morning,
more than watchmen wait for the morning.
7 Israel, put your hope in the LORD,
for with the LORD is unfailing love
and with him is full redemption.
8 He himself will redeem Israel
from all their sins.

The result of confession = forgiveness.

God offers these things to those who repent.

REFLECTION QUESTIONS

As you practice confession, what are the benefits you can remember that will help you keep going even when you don't want to?

Look especially at verse 5 of Psalm 130. How do these words encourage you, especially when you struggle to break a sin pattern in your life?

PRAYER PRACTICE

Write a prayer below confessing your own imperfection and praising the greatness of God. Thank Him for Jesus and the beauty of forgiveness.

WEEK TWO

WEEKEND REFLECTION

When Jesus taught His disciples to pray, He taught them to confess: *"And forgive us our debts, as we also have forgiven our debtors"* (Matthew 6:12).

Part of our daily rhythm of prayer is meant to include confession. Both the New Testament and the Old Testament make it clear that asking for forgiveness and acknowledging our sin is key, according to Jesus. Letting ourselves be searched and known by God deepens our intimacy with Him. (Psalm 139:23-24) We do not have to hide in shame. He has forgiven us and will forgive us because of what Jesus did on the cross!

Jesus also teaches us to forgive one another. But that word "forgiveness" is complicated. It's one thing to receive the forgiveness Jesus so freely offers, but it's also sometimes challenging to consider where we may need to extend forgiveness to someone else. Especially when someone has deeply wounded us with their words, betrayed us or broken our trust.

But just as our confession opens the door to forgiveness from God, we need to make space for it to open up forgiveness with others.

As you pray and think through this, consider the words of Colossians 3:12-14: *"Therefore, as God's chosen people, holy and dearly loved, clothe yourselves with compassion, kindness, humility, gentleness and patience. Bear with each other and forgive one another if any of you has a grievance against someone. Forgive as the Lord forgave you. And over all these virtues put on love, which binds them all together in perfect unity."*

A PRAYER FOR YOU

God, thank You that when I confess my sins, shortcomings and failures to You, You are faithful and just to forgive me, cleanse me and make me new. Just like David asked in Psalm 51, I ask You to make my heart pure. Help me to flee from temptation and choose righteousness. Remind me of the gift of Your grace, and show me how to extend that grace to others — because no matter what they've done or will do, no one is too far away for Your mercy and love to reach. In Jesus' name, amen.

WEEK THREE

PRAYERS OF THANKSGIVING

A prayer of David.

1 Hear me, LORD, and answer me,
for I am poor and needy.
2 Guard my life, for I am faithful to you;
save your servant who trusts in you.
You are my God; 3 have mercy on me, Lord,
for I call to you all day long.
4 Bring joy to your servant, Lord,
for I put my trust in you.
5 You, Lord, are forgiving and good,
abounding in love to all who call to you.
6 Hear my prayer, LORD;
listen to my cry for mercy.
7 When I am in distress, I call to you,
because you answer me.
8 Among the gods there is none like you, Lord;
no deeds can compare with yours.
9 All the nations you have made
will come and worship before you, Lord;
they will bring glory to your name.
10 For you are great and do marvelous deeds;
you alone are God.
11 Teach me your way, LORD,
that I may rely on your faithfulness;
give me an undivided heart,
that I may fear your name.
12 I will praise you, Lord my God, with all my heart;
I will glorify your name forever.
13 For great is your love toward me;
you have delivered me from the depths,
from the realm of the dead.
14 Arrogant foes are attacking me, O God;
ruthless people are trying to kill me—
they have no regard for you.
15 But you, Lord, are a compassionate and gracious God,
slow to anger, abounding in love and faithfulness.
16 Turn to me and have mercy on me;
show your strength in behalf of your servant;
save me, because I serve you
just as my mother did.
17 Give me a sign of your goodness,
that my enemies may see it and be put to shame,
for you, LORD, have helped me and comforted me.

DAY 11

God's Steadfast Love

For the woman who needs to be reminded of God's steadfast love for her.

SHELBY DIXON AND MARY BOSWELL

TODAY'S READING: Psalm 86

MAJOR MOMENT: His life in danger, David asked God to preserve him and thanked God for His steadfast love.

KEY VERSES: Psalm 86:6-7

Hear my prayer, LORD; listen to my cry for mercy.
When I am in distress, I call to you, because you answer me.

In Psalm 86, "A Prayer of David," we get an intimate glimpse at a conversation between God and King David. David gives us a beautiful example of how to pray with thanksgiving, our prayer focus for this week. Psalm 86 is the only Davidic prayer in a section of Psalms that some scholars call the "book of crisis." But we'll study it today as a psalm of thanksgiving. Thanksgiving in crisis may sound like a contradiction ... but somehow David reconciled gratitude and grief in his prayer, and that means we can too.

How is thanksgiving different from adoration (which we learned about during Week 1 of this study)? Recall these definitions from Day 1: "Adoration is praise that originates from our hearts and that we pour out on God. Thanksgiving is our response to the love, blessing and compassion that flows from God onto us."

Adoration	PRAISE THAT ORIGINATES FROM OUR HEARTS AND THAT WE POUR OUT ON GOD
Thanksgiving	OUR RESPONSE TO THE LOVE, BLESSING AND COMPASSION THAT FLOWS FROM GOD ONTO US

Although we don't know the exact source of his trouble in this passage, we do know that through his prayer, David demonstrated how we can ask God for help while also thanking Him. Let's dive in so we can learn to pray with thanksgiving even when we're afraid, desperate and in need of a miracle.

In verses 1-7, David asked eight things of God. What are they?

1.

2.

3.

4.

5.

6.

7.

8.

It's surprising that David started a prayer of thanksgiving with eight requests of God. Because of this approach, what can we learn about the nature or format of prayers of thanksgiving?

What does this reveal about God?

In verses 8-13, David shifted from petitioning God to praising Him for His power. At this point in the psalm, David hasn't explicitly thanked God for anything. Even though the word "thanks" is not used explicitly by David, we can start to see threads of thanksgiving woven through David's desperate appeal. How so? First, we need to understand something about thankfulness.

Thanksgiving is rooted in looking first at the past and then at the present. We can look at what God has done for us (and for others, like David) while also deciphering His hand in our lives right now.

With that in mind, what do you see that makes this a prayer/psalm of thanksgiving?

What signs of thanksgiving do you see? List the verses here:

Twice, David looked at what God had done in the past: *"all the nations **you have** made"* (v. 9) and *"**you have** delivered me from the depths, from the realm of the dead"* (v. 13, emphasis added). These two past-tense acts of God serve as reminders that:

1. Because God made all the nations, He made the very men who were *"attacking"* and *"trying to kill"* David (v. 14). Could He not then thwart their efforts to kill David? What's more, David says all nations *"will come and worship before you, Lord"* (v. 9). One day, every knee will bow before God. (Philippians 2:10-11)

2. God had saved David's soul from Sheol, the realm of the dead. His soul settled, David did not need to fear physical harm or death.

This is not the only time David called out to the Lord. In Psalm 3, which scholars estimate was written before Psalm 86, we see one example when David praised the Lord for being *"a shield around [him], [his] glory, the One who lifts [his] head high"* (Psalm 3:3). Because the Lord had previously met David in a personal way, David could confidently thank God for His intimate, steadfast love and for His forgiveness, mercy and faithfulness in this current time of need (Psalm 86:5; Psalm 86:15).

NOTE FROM JOEL

The realm of the dead = Sheol.

The Ancient Israelites believed death took place when the human soul separated from the body. The body decayed while the soul went to Sheol (לואְש). In the Old Testament, Sheol referred to the place where both the righteous dead (like Jacob in Genesis 37:35 or Samuel in 1 Samuel 28:13-14) and the wicked dead (Psalm 31:17) would go. However, the righteous and wicked are located in two different places within Sheol.

These two locations are *"Hades,"* where the wicked suffer (Luke 16:23), and what the Bible refers to as *"Abraham's side"* (Luke 16:22), which seems to be a place of rest for the righteous as they await the Messiah, Jesus. It's interesting that there is even a *"great chasm"* or divide between the two places (Luke 16:26).

HADES	GREAT CHASM	ABRAHAM'S SIDE
where the wicked suffer *Luke 16:23*	*Luke 16:26*	a place of rest for the righteous as they await the Messiah *Luke 16:22*

David also looked at who God is in the present: *"Among the gods there* **is** *none like you, Lord;*
no deeds **can** *compare with yours"* (v. 8, emphasis added).

Wrapping up his prayer, David offered a sneak peek of his complete trust in God for his deliverance. He also asked for a tangible sign of God's goodness so his enemies would see it and know God was at work.

Why do you think it might be important to pray for others to see or come to see God's work in our lives?

How have you experienced and shared God's steadfast love with others?

David realized his great need for God. He prayed and asked God to guide him so he could follow His faithful, divine instruction. In doing so, David longed for his heart to be joined with God's in reverence and honor. Bible commentator David Guzik states that David's realization "brought him to say, 'Don't give me my way, Lord; teach me Your way.'" And as David lived out that prayer, he became known as a man after God's heart (1 Samuel 13:14; Acts 13:22).

How can you model your prayers after this one? What words or phrases can you use in your own prayers?

PRAYER PRACTICE

Today, write your prayer of thanksgiving using Psalm 86 as a guide. Recall a time in the past when God came to your rescue, and review details of His deliverance in your prayer, letting God's past faithfulness guide you to thanksgiving.

Of David.

1 Contend, LORD, with those who contend with me;
fight against those who fight against me.
2 Take up shield and armor;
arise and come to my aid.
3 Brandish spear and javelin
against those who pursue me.
Say to me,
"I am your salvation."
4 May those who seek my life
be disgraced and put to shame;
may those who plot my ruin
be turned back in dismay.
5 May they be like chaff before the wind,
with the angel of the LORD driving them away;
6 may their path be dark and slippery,
with the angel of the LORD pursuing them.
7 Since they hid their net for me without cause
and without cause dug a pit for me,
8 may ruin overtake them by surprise—
may the net they hid entangle them,
may they fall into the pit, to their ruin.
9 Then my soul will rejoice in the LORD
and delight in his salvation.
10 My whole being will exclaim,
"Who is like you, LORD?
You rescue the poor from those too strong for them,
the poor and needy from those who rob them."
11 Ruthless witnesses come forward;
they question me on things I know nothing about.
12 They repay me evil for good
and leave me like one bereaved.
13 Yet when they were ill, I put on sackcloth
and humbled myself with fasting.
When my prayers returned to me unanswered,
14 I went about mourning
as though for my friend or brother.
I bowed my head in grief
as though weeping for my mother.
15 But when I stumbled, they gathered in glee;
assailants gathered against me without my knowledge.
They slandered me without ceasing.
16 Like the ungodly they maliciously mocked;
they gnashed their teeth at me.

17 How long, Lord, will you look on?
Rescue me from their ravages,
my precious life from these lions.
18 I will give you thanks in the great assembly;
among the throngs I will praise you.
19 Do not let those gloat over me
who are my enemies without cause;
do not let those who hate me without reason
maliciously wink the eye.
20 They do not speak peaceably,
but devise false accusations
against those who live quietly in the land.
21 They sneer at me and say, "Aha! Aha!
With our own eyes we have seen it."
22 LORD, you have seen this; do not be silent.
Do not be far from me, Lord.
23 Awake, and rise to my defense!
Contend for me, my God and Lord.
24 Vindicate me in your righteousness, LORD
my God;
do not let them gloat over me.
25 Do not let them think, "Aha, just what we
wanted!"
or say, "We have swallowed him up."
26 May all who gloat over my distress
be put to shame and confusion;
may all who exalt themselves over me
be clothed with shame and disgrace.
27 May those who delight in my vindication
shout for joy and gladness;
may they always say, "The LORD be exalted,
who delights in the well-being of his ser-
vant."
28 My tongue will proclaim your righteous-
ness,
your praises all day long.

DAY 12

Giving Thanks Even in Betrayal

For the woman who needs to remember God is her protector.

SHELBY DIXON AND SARAH FRAZER

TODAY'S READING: Psalm 35

MAJOR MOMENT: David cried out for God to protect him against those who betrayed him.

KEY VERSE: Psalm 35:18

I will give you thanks in the great assembly; among the throngs I will praise you.

At some point, we've all felt the sting of betrayal by someone we love. David did, too — and he let that sting drive him to cry out to God, who fights for us and will ultimately enact justice. Today we'll dig into David's prayer of thanksgiving to the God *"who delights in the well-being of his servant"* (Psalm 35:27).

In Psalm 35, David was under attack again — this time by men who sought to destroy him when he'd done nothing wrong. David's prayer reveals these were people he'd cared about at one time, (vv. 13-14) making their betrayal even more heartbreaking.

> Verses 1-3 are full of war language. Jot down the battle terms you notice. What was David asking God to be and do for him?

The first word in this psalm, *"contend,"* actually referred to legal matters in Hebrew (Psalm 35:1). By using this word, David reminds us God is not only our Advocate but also our Judge. David's enemies were testifying falsely about him (Psalm 35:11; Psalm 35:20), but David didn't just idly hope the truth would come out. He prayed for God to bring justice, and in faith, he thanked God even when others might have been believing lies about him.

Just like Psalm 86, this dark psalm doesn't seem like a prayer of thanksgiving. It certainly reflects real life, which is often a mix of happiness and heartbreak. Still, we can always thank God because thanksgiving is an act of worship not dependent on our circumstances. Often, our prayers might sound like David's as we pour out our hearts while acknowledging what is true about God.

Think of a time when you experienced heartbreaking circumstances. How did thanksgiving change your perspective of the situation? Or how could thanksgiving change your perspective now, looking back?

Circumstance	CHANGE OF PERSPECTIVE THROUGH THANKSGIVING

In this psalm, we see David giving thanks for God's heart for the poor, needy and weak. (vv. 9-10, 22-24) There are three instances of thanksgiving woven into David's pleas for deliverance, his lament over his enemies' hatred, and his petition for justice. These instances are tied to his body and soul, location, and time:

BODY AND SOUL

"My whole being" refers to wholehearted praise and joy. David's bones and his very soul rejoiced at the Lord's salvation. (vv. 9-10)

LOCATION

Once God saved David from his enemies, David promised to offer thanksgiving not only in private but in community, so others would come to know of God's deliverance and have the opportunity to trust Him. (v. 18)

TIME

David also promised to thank God continually.
David would not soon forget God's deliverance. (v. 28)

List some ways you can thank God, your protector ...

With your whole body and soul:

In community:

Continually:

Let's look at verse 27. What was David hoping would happen?

Who would be glorified by this situation?

Even when others hate us, or just dislike us, *"without cause"* (vv. 7, 19), the Lord delights in our well-being, our happiness and our security. As you pray whispers of thanksgiving to God this week, you may also consider repeating the words of Psalm 91:2 (GNT): *"You are my defender and protector. You are my God; in you I trust."*

God does not forget His people, and He says all will be made right (Psalm 103:6; Jeremiah 9:24). God's character is the foundation for giving thanks. David acknowledged that *"LORD, you have seen this"* (Psalm 35:22); God does not overlook or miss what is happening to us. David was so confident of this that he prayed others would join him in saying, *"Great is the LORD, who delights in the welfare of his servant!"* (Psalm 35:27, ESV). The word "welfare" means peace and completeness, especially in relationship with God.

David invites us to *"shout for joy and gladness"* (Psalm 35:27) because of God's great salvation. Although we might feel powerless and voiceless, our hearts can rise up in prayers of thanksgiving because our God sees, cares for and defends us. Even in betrayal, we can give thanks. We give thanks not for the betrayal but for God's character, care and concern for us.

PRAYER PRACTICE

Think of a time when you were betrayed. Craft a prayer thanking God for His comfort during that time, and if applicable, for the result afterward.

PSALM 100

A psalm. For giving grateful praise.

1 Shout for joy to the LORD, all the earth.
2 Worship the LORD with gladness;
come before him with joyful songs.
3 Know that the LORD is God.
It is he who made us, and we are his;
we are his people, the sheep of his pasture.
4 Enter his gates with thanksgiving
and his courts with praise;
give thanks to him and praise his name.
5 For the LORD is good and his love endures forever;
his faithfulness continues through all generations.

DAY 13

My Creator and Shepherd

For the woman who needs to know she belongs to God.

SHELBY DIXON AND MICAH MADDOX

TODAY'S READING: Psalm 100

MAJOR MOMENT: God's people are invited to make a joyful noise of thanksgiving.

KEY VERSE: Psalm 100:3

Know that the LORD is God. It is he who made us, and we are his;
we are his people, the sheep of his pasture.

Psalm 100 is a little different than ones we have previously studied. It is the only psalm in Scripture with the specific subtitle "For giving grateful praise." At least theoretically, we know we should be thankful and praise the Lord, but the key to thanksgiving, as we'll learn in today's psalm, is knowing why we should thank God, even when life is hard and we are tempted to forget how good He really is.

Thanksgiving is woven into the fabric of what we believe about ourselves and about God.

ABOUT THIS PSALM

First, Psalm 100 is not attributed to David like the last two we've studied. Some Old Testament scholars attribute this psalm to Moses, but there are questions surrounding its authorship.[1]

Secondly, this psalm doesn't address the Lord directly, though it still holds elements of prayer. Verses 1, 2 and 4 are **invitations** to God's people while verses 3 and 5 describe both believers and the Lord.

Finally, Psalm 100 reflects a subtype of thanksgiving psalms called "enthronement psalms," which include Psalms 47, 93 and 95-99 (so we studied another enthronement psalm, Psalm 95, in Week 1).[2] Enthronement psalms are directly connected to corporate worship.

In verse 1, who does Psalm 100 address? We can think of this as the "invitee." (Also see similar examples in Psalm 96:1, Psalm 97:1 and Psalm 98:4.)

There is an invitation in Psalm 100:1 that calls the entire earth to come to the Lord with thanksgiving and worship. This is not a psalm written just for a private moment of meditation or a one-on-one prayer alone with God. It is a psalm written for the masses to join together in unified thanks and loud praise to the Lord!

The first four verses give a series of directives or exaltations that are each qualified with the manner in which we should respond.

Go to the psalm and circle the verbs in each statement of verses 1-4.

Now underline the qualifying phrases for each action.

Fill in the following chart:

ACTION / VERB	HOW / QUALIFIER	WHO / RESPONDANT
Shout to the Lord	*With joy*	*All the earth*

So often, we read Scripture as if for our own edification or learning, but this psalm is particularly calling us to think of the greater body of which we are part. The psalmist gives us the reasons for this worldwide worship in verses three and five.

Psalm 100:3 says, *"Know that the LORD is God. It is he who made us, and we are his; we are his people, the sheep of his pasture."*

Within this verse, we find two amazing characterizations of God:

God is the Creator.
AND
God is the Shepherd.

These are foundational to our identity in Him. When we know who we come from (our Creator God) and who we are walking with if we are following Jesus (the Lord our Shepherd), we desire to thank Him because of who He is and because we are His. This is when sincere thanksgiving is born in a believer's heart.

Knowing *about* God and knowing God *personally* produce different responses.

James 2:19 tells us, *"even the demons believe ... and shudder"* that God exists. But when we truly know we are His and invest in a personal relationship with Him, our prayers overflow with praise and thanksgiving ... and in the case of Psalm 100, loud, corporate thanksgiving together with other believers.

What does verse 3 teach us about who God is?

What does it say about who we are to God?

What do verses 1-4 teach us about how we are to respond to God?

What is the posture of your heart as you pray, worship, serve, and enter into the presence of God?

In what ways might you change how you are going to God in prayer to experience a deeper sense of gladness and thanksgiving?

Psalm 100:4 says, *"Enter his gates with thanksgiving and his courts with praise; give thanks to him and praise his name."* There is only one reason we as believers can enter God's presence so freely, so boldly.

In Hebrews 10:17-19, God tells us: *"'Their sins and lawless acts I will remember no more.' And where these have been forgiven, sacrifice for sin is no longer necessary. Therefore, brothers and sisters, since we have confidence to enter the Most Holy Place by the blood of Jesus."*

It is incredible to think that the writer of Psalm 100 praised God so fervently even before Jesus came to live, die and resurrect on earth. How much more reason do we have to thank Him today when we open our Bibles and read the entire gospel! Jesus is worthy of loud, resounding gratitude and praise like we read about in Psalm 100.

God is so much more than we can wrap our minds around. While we study His Word and remember who He is, may we always stay in majestic awe of His goodness. He didn't have to let us into His presence, but in His everlasting mercy, He loves us and allows us to become part of His family forever through faith in Jesus.

Our psalm today ends with all the reason we could ever need for worship, praise, thanksgiving, service and prayer:

For the LORD is good and his love endures forever;
his faithfulness continues through all generations. (Psalm 100:5)

God's goodness in and of itself is cause for gratitude. But the final phrases in this verse especially hit home why we owe God thanks for His magnificent goodness: because His love doesn't depend on *our* goodness. His love is free. It is forever. And we can rest in His faithfulness.

Even if life feels difficult right now or circumstances seem dark, we can remember we are created by God and shepherded by Him. Then, in a spirit of thanksgiving, we can come to Him in prayer, declaring the truth about His goodness, unending love and faithfulness. It's something worth *"shout[ing] for joy"* about (Psalm 100:1)! This might mean you sing a little louder at church, crank up the praise music, or make more time for praying together with your family. No matter what it looks like, God's people are called to give Him thanks simply because we are His, and He is ours.

How does it make you feel to know God's love never ends and He doesn't discriminate when it comes to His faithfulness?

NOTE FROM JOEL
ENTHRONMENT PSALMS

Psalms directly connected to corporate worship

Includes Psalms 47, 93, 95, 96, 97, 98, 99

Yahweh is the only King.

Set the stage for our understanding of the enthronement of King Jesus. (Romans 8:34)

Reflect our modern songs of Jesus King forever!

PRAYER PRACTICE

Finish writing the prayer of thanksgiving below, using the language of Psalm 100.

Dear God, You are my Creator and my Shepherd. With the rest of creation, I join in making a joyful noise to You today. Help me to serve You with gladness because of who You are and what You've done for me, knowing that it is an act of worship ...

1 Give thanks to the LORD, for he is good;
his love endures forever.

2 Let the redeemed of the LORD tell their story—
those he redeemed from the hand of the foe,
3 those he gathered from the lands,
from east and west, from north and south.

4 Some wandered in desert wastelands,
finding no way to a city where they could settle.
5 They were hungry and thirsty,
and their lives ebbed away.
6 Then they cried out to the LORD in their trouble,
and he delivered them from their distress.
7 He led them by a straight way
to a city where they could settle.
8 Let them give thanks to the LORD for his unfailing love
and his wonderful deeds for mankind,
9 for he satisfies the thirsty
and fills the hungry with good things.

10 Some sat in darkness, in utter darkness,
prisoners suffering in iron chains,
11 because they rebelled against God's commands
and despised the plans of the Most High.
12 So he subjected them to bitter labor;
they stumbled, and there was no one to help.
13 Then they cried to the LORD in their trouble,
and he saved them from their distress.
14 He brought them out of darkness, the utter darkness,
and broke away their chains.
15 Let them give thanks to the LORD for his unfailing love
and his wonderful deeds for mankind,
16 for he breaks down gates of bronze
and cuts through bars of iron.

17 Some became fools through their rebellious ways
and suffered affliction because of their iniquities.
18 They loathed all food
and drew near the gates of death.
19 Then they cried to the LORD in their trouble,
and he saved them from their distress.
20 He sent out his word and healed them;
he rescued them from the grave.
21 Let them give thanks to the LORD for his unfailing love
and his wonderful deeds for mankind.
22 Let them sacrifice thank offerings
and tell of his works with songs of joy.

23 Some went out on the sea in ships;
they were merchants on the mighty waters.
24 They saw the works of the LORD,
his wonderful deeds in the deep.
25 For he spoke and stirred up a tempest
that lifted high the waves.
26 They mounted up to the heavens and went down to the depths;
in their peril their courage melted away.
27 They reeled and staggered like drunkards;
they were at their wits' end.
28 Then they cried out to the LORD in their trouble,
and he brought them out of their distress.
29 He stilled the storm to a whisper;
the waves of the sea were hushed.
30 They were glad when it grew calm,
and he guided them to their desired haven.
31 Let them give thanks to the LORD for his unfailing love
and his wonderful deeds for mankind.
32 Let them exalt him in the assembly of the people
and praise him in the council of the elders.

33 He turned rivers into a desert,
flowing springs into thirsty ground,
34 and fruitful land into a salt waste,
because of the wickedness of those who lived there.
35 He turned the desert into pools of water
and the parched ground into flowing springs;
36 there he brought the hungry to live,
and they founded a city where they could settle.
37 They sowed fields and planted vineyards
that yielded a fruitful harvest;
38 he blessed them, and their numbers greatly increased,
and he did not let their herds diminish.

39 Then their numbers decreased, and they were humbled
by oppression, calamity and sorrow;
40 he who pours contempt on nobles
made them wander in a trackless waste.
41 But he lifted the needy out of their affliction
and increased their families like flocks.
42 The upright see and rejoice,
but all the wicked shut their mouths.

43 Let the one who is wise heed these things
and ponder the loving deeds of the LORD.

DAY 14

The Steadfast Love of the Lord

For the woman who needs reminding that God delivers and redeems.

SHELBY DIXON AND LISA ALVIN-MEYER

TODAY'S READING: Psalm 107

MAJOR MOMENT: A psalmist testified to God's rescue in trouble and His sovereignty over nature, governments and all peoples.

KEY VERSES: Psalm 107:1-2

Give thanks to the LORD, for he is good;
his love endures forever.
Let the redeemed of the LORD tell their story—
those he redeemed from the hand of the foe.

With 43 verses, Psalm 107 is the longest psalm we'll study this week. It may have been written during the Babylonian exile and features four testimonies of God's deliverance of His people.[1] In today's Scripture passage, we find four groups of people who may have taken the idea of "helping themselves" too literally, until they were helpless before God. The opening verses of Psalm 107 set a tone of thanksgiving for the entire psalm (vv. 1-2). But the psalm then paints four poetic illustrations of people in distress. Not only can we be encouraged by these testaments to God's power and dominion, but we can also learn how to model our prayers of thanksgiving after this one.

Read Psalm 107:4-32. What patterns do you notice among the four testimonies shared here? What did God deliver each group of people from?

Those who wandered:

Those who sat in darkness:

Those who were foolish:

Those who sailed:

Each of these groups reached what we might call "rock bottom": the lowest possible point, given their circumstances. All their human wisdom, resources and initiative failed, and they came to the end of their self-sufficiency. When they accepted there was nothing left they could do, they cried out to God in prayer, and He delivered/saved them from *"their distress"* (vv. 6, 13, 19, 28).

The psalmist shares:

- **What God did in each situation.** For example: *"He led [the wanderers] by a straight way to a city where they could settle"* (v. 7).
- **What we're to do in response to God.** For example: *"Let them give thanks to the LORD for his unfailing love and his wonderful deeds for mankind"* (v. 8).
- **Why our lives should overflow with gratitude for God.** For example: *"He satisfies the thirsty and fills the hungry with good things"* (v. 9).

> Which testimony of God's deliverance resonates with you the most? What kind of deliverance do you need right now?

Many commentators believe this psalm refers historically to God's redemption of Israel from their exile in Babylon (2 Kings 24:14; 1 Chronicles 9:1b), yet its relevance is also timeless. Just as God answered each group's desperate cry for help, He will do the same for us today. Whether we feel like a wanderer, prisoner, fool or sailor in a storm, when we come to the end of our self-sufficiency, our Lord of infinite grace and mercy will deliver us and supply everything we need ... if only we will humbly call upon Him (Psalm 50:15; Philippians 4:19).

In the second and third testimonies (vv. 10-16, 17-22), we find the people experiencing crises caused by their own sin. Still, when they cried out to God in repentance, He delivered them just as He delivered the people in verses 6 and 28.

> In what circumstances past or present can you relate to crises caused in some way by your own sin?

We are never too far gone for God to save us, and even when we walk through difficulties of our own making, He is faithful to rescue us. What a beautiful picture of God's mercy and grace!

If thankfulness is cultivated by looking at God's faithfulness in the past, as we learned on Day 11, and if this Psalm 107 prayer was indeed written during Israel's exile in Babylon, what event in Israel's history might verses 4-9 be about? And what about verses 23-32?

PSALM 107 SCRIPTURES	COMMONALITIES	EVENTS BEFORE BABYLONIAN EXILE
Verses 4-9		Numbers 32:13; Deuteronomy 1:6-8
Verses 23-32		Jonah 1:4-15; Jonah 2

The last 10 verses of the Psalm 107 prayer are about God's dominion over nature, people and governments. Not only does He care for the hungry, poor and needy, but He also executes justice on those who oppress them. This language is similar to David's in Psalm 86 and Psalm 35.

How can you model your prayers after Psalm 107?

Praying words of gratitude to God Himself, telling others about what God has done in our lives is a way to put our thanksgiving into action. Every time we testify, we plant seeds of hope that the Holy Spirit can use to change lives for God's glory.

What words or phrases can you use in your own prayers?

PRAYER PRACTICE

Write your own prayer of thanksgiving today by *"ponder[ing] the loving deeds of the* LORD*"* in your life (Psalm 107:43). Think about your testimony, how God saved you and brought you into His family and delivered you from crisis. Then form a prayer of thanksgiving modeled after the pattern of the four testimonies in Psalm 107, beginning with your crisis, how you cried out to God, and what He did to deliver you. End your prayer by thanking God for His steadfast love and for what you've experienced through His deliverance.

Of David.

1 I will praise you, LORD, with all my heart;
before the "gods" I will sing your praise.
2 I will bow down toward your holy temple
and will praise your name
for your unfailing love and your faithfulness,
for you have so exalted your solemn decree
that it surpasses your fame.
3 When I called, you answered me;
you greatly emboldened me.

4 May all the kings of the earth praise you, LORD,
when they hear what you have decreed.
5 May they sing of the ways of the LORD,
for the glory of the LORD is great.

6 Though the LORD is exalted, he looks kindly on the lowly;
though lofty, he sees them from afar.
7 Though I walk in the midst of trouble,
you preserve my life.
You stretch out your hand against the anger of my foes;
with your right hand you save me.
8 The LORD will vindicate me;
your love, LORD, endures forever—
do not abandon the works of your hands.

DAY 15

Thanking God for the Past, Present and Future

For the woman thanking God for answered prayer and asking for His continued faithfulness.

SHELBY DIXON AND ANDREA CHATELAIN

TODAY'S READING: Psalm 138

MAJOR MOMENT: David publicly and wholeheartedly thanked God for answered prayer.

KEY VERSE: Psalm 138:1
I will praise you, LORD, with all my heart;
before the "gods" I will sing your praise.

Today, let's read Psalm 138 together. We've included the text of the psalm right here in your study guide, and we've made some notes on verses 1-3 to get you started; take some time to annotate Psalm 138:4-8 yourself! There's no right or wrong way to do this, so let Scripture and the Holy Spirit guide you to notice, circle, underline, highlight and make note of anything God wants to teach you. Then thoughtfully consider the reflection questions below, ending with your own prayer of thanksgiving.

PSALM 138

Of David.

1 I will praise you, LORD, with all my heart;
before the "gods" I will sing your praise.
2 I will bow down toward your holy temple
and will praise your name
for your unfailing love and your faithfulness,
for you have so exalted your solemn decree
that it surpasses your fame.
3 When I called, you answered me;
you greatly emboldened me.

NOTES

All my heart = not partial praise

David's actions:
-give
-bow down
-sing
-call

See Psalm 108:4, Psalm 115:1 and Psalm 117:2. Verse 1: "'Gods' could refer to the pagan gods, in which case David was praising the true God in spite of their supposed presence."[1]

Answered prayer!

4 May all the kings of the earth praise you, LORD,
when they hear what you have decreed.
5 May they sing of the ways of the LORD,
for the glory of the Lord is great.

6 Though the LORD is exalted, he looks kindly on the lowly;
though lofty, he sees them from afar.
7 Though I walk in the midst of trouble,
you preserve my life.
You stretch out your hand against the anger of my foes;
with your right hand you save me.
8 The LORD will vindicate me;
your love, LORD, endures forever—
do not abandon the works of your hands.

NOTES

COSMIC NATURE OF PSALM 138

Verse 1 *"before the 'gods'"*	the gods = elohim, Septuagint(LXX) translates the Hebrew elohim as "angels" (ἀγγέλων)
Verse 2 *"I will bow down toward your holy temple and will praise your name."*	• God is King of heaven and earth • Temple is throne room of God • Supernatural beings singing constant praise to God (Isaiah 6:1-4)

As a boy, David went out to face Goliath, a mighty Philistine. Goliath took one look at David and cursed him in the name of his *"gods"* (1 Samuel 17:43). At this moment, David may have remembered how the Philistines stole the Ark of the Covenant from God's people years ago and set the Ark next to a statue of their god Dagon. But God caused Dagon to fall down twice overnight in a posture of defeat before the Ark of the Covenant (1 Samuel 5:1-5). David knew his God's name was greater than that of any other gods, nations or kings (Psalm 138:1; Psalm 138:4). So he told Goliath, *"I come against you in the name of the LORD Almighty, the God of the armies of Israel"* (1 Samuel 17:45). And in Psalm 138, David prayed his thanks to the Lord in the presence of all heavenly beings and any other so-called "gods" from other nations. Unlike the statue of Dagon, David *willingly* bowed to Yahweh in reverence and gratitude (Psalm 138:2).

In this prayer, David is thankful *in* the name of his God and *for* the name of his God. But it's not the first time we glimpse his confidence in the power of God's name above all others ...

What does praying thanks *in* the name of God mean to you?

What does praying thanks *for* the name of God mean as well? What is the difference?

As we've seen throughout our study of Psalms, there were times in David's life when he felt pretty low. In Psalm 138, we read David's description of God: *"Though the LORD is exalted, he looks kindly on the lowly; though lofty, he sees them from afar"* (Psalm 138:6).

The Hebrew word for "lowly" is שָׁפָל *(shaphal),* meaning "low in station or humble in condition or spirit." David asserted that Yaweh, the God more powerful than any other, sees and cares for those who we would say are too low in status for His attention. And He sees those whose circumstances have brought them low.

What does Jesus say about when we feel this way? In one of His most famous teachings, the Sermon on the Mount, *"He began to teach them .... 'Blessed are the poor in spirit, for theirs is the kingdom of heaven"* (Matthew 5:2-3).

When you feel so lowly and poor in spirit that God seems far off, be reminded by Psalm 138 and Matthew 5 that He is near to the lowly. And soak in your Savior's words:

He has elevated you by His sacrifice to be worthy of His Kingdom.
You are important to Jesus.

REFLECTION QUESTIONS

David starts this prayer of thanksgiving by explaining how he praises God and then goes on to share what God has done. This order is not a natural cause-and-effect relationship of "God did this; therefore, I'll praise Him." Why do you think that is? What does this say about when and why we should give thanks to God?

Read Psalm 138:7 and Psalm 23:4, both written by David. How are these verses similar?

What language of thanksgiving stands out to you in Psalm 138? What verse do you find most significant, and why?

PRAYER PRACTICE

Consider how faithful and true the Lord your God was to David, and how David's prayers give us a firsthand account of relationship with God.

Write your own prayer of thanksgiving to God whether you are feeling full or less than right now. Practice prayer of thanksgiving in spite of and because of your circumstances.

WEEK THREE

WEEKEND REFLECTION

This week, as we've studied prayers of thanksgiving in the book of Psalm, we've learned ...

- God loves us with a steadfast love. (Psalm 86)
- God protects us at all times, even when we're under attack by those who've betrayed us. (Psalm 35)
- God holds us in the palm of His hand because we belong to Him. (Psalm 100)
- God delivers and redeems us no matter what we're going through. (Psalm 107)
- God answers prayer and will always be faithful to us. (Psalm 138)

All of these are reasons to give thanks to God. But we've also learned that thanksgiving is not dependent on our circumstances; it's an act of worship (remember this from Day 12?). We may be in the middle of a terrible situation — maybe even one caused by our own sin (as we discussed on Day 14) — but we can still give wholehearted thanks to God because of what He's done in the past and what He's currently doing now, even when we can't see it. As we learned on Day 11: **Thanksgiving is rooted in looking first at the past and then at the present. We can look at what God *has done* for us (and for others) while also deciphering His hand in our lives *right now*.**

How can we not feel thankful when we dwell on who God is to us, who we are to God, and the beautifully astounding fact that we can have a personal relationship with our loving, merciful Creator?!

After all, as we learned on Day 13, a right perspective about our relationship with God helps to get our hearts in the right posture for thanksgiving. That kind of thanksgiving is offered with *"my whole being,"* as David says in Psalm 35:10. Even if the bad situation we're walking through was caused by our own sin, we are never too far gone for God, and He is faithful.

Let us pray a prayer of thanksgiving over you, composed of verses from our thanksgiving psalms, to close out our week of study.

A PRAYER FOR YOU

Dear Lord, You are good and forgiving, abounding in steadfast love to all who call upon You. You are great and do wondrous things, and You alone are God. "For great is your love toward me ...." *(Psalm 86:13) I cry out to You in my trouble, confessing the ways I've rebelled against Your words. (Psalm 107) At the same time, my soul rejoices in You, exulting in Your salvation.* "I will give you thanks in the great assembly; among the throngs I will praise you." *(Psalm 35:18) May all the earth make a joyful noise to You; may we serve You with gladness and come into Your presence with singing! (Psalm 100:1–3) Though I walk in the midst of trouble, please preserve my life.* "Do not abandon the work of your hands." *(Psalm 138:8b) In Jesus' name, amen.*

Word Study of *Yada* (Hebrew for "Give Thanks")

The Hebrew verb for "give thanks" is *yada* (pronounced "yaw-daw"). Generally, it means "to throw, shoot, or cast," but in specific contexts, it can mean "to give thanks or praise," also "to confess sin." Yada is related to the noun *yad* -"hand."

How is thanksgiving related to our hands?

Think of how we raise or extend our hands in praise and worship. When we praise God, throwing our hands up, we are thanking Him for who He is and what He's done as well as declaring in faith what we believe He'll do in the future.

Yada appears 114 times in the Old Testament—and the book of Psalms contains 64 instances of *yada*. **That's more than half of all the biblical usages!**

There are two notable instances of yada outside of psalms. One is when Leah, the wife of Jacob, birthed her fourth son, Judah, saying, *"This time I will praise [yada] the LORD"* (Genesis 29:35a).

The second is when David prayed his song of praise for being delivered from Saul in 2 Samuel 22 David said: *"Therefore I will praise [yada] you, LORD, among the nations; I will sing the praises of your name"* (2 Samuel 22:50).

Psalms in this study that include the word yada and the corresponding weeks you'll study those psalms:

WEEK 1

"All your works **praise** *you,* L*ORD;*
your faithful people extol you." Psalm 145:10, emphasis added

WEEK 2

"Then I acknowledged my sin to you
and did not cover up my iniquity.
*I said, '***I will confess**
my transgressions to the L*ORD.'*
And you forgave
the guilt of my sin." Psalm 32:5, emphasis added

WEEK 3

"I will give you thanks *in the great assembly;*
among the throngs I will praise you." Psalm 35:18, emphasis added
*"...***give thanks** *to him and praise his name."* Psalm 100:4b, emphasis added
"Give thanks to the L*ORD, for he is good;*
his love endures forever." Psalm 107:1, emphasis added
"Let them give thanks *to the* L*ORD for his unfailing love*
and his wonderful deeds for mankind" Psalm 107:8, 15, 21, 31, emphasis added
"I will **praise you,** L*ORD, with all my heart;*
before the 'gods' I will sing your praise.... " Psalm 138:1, emphasis added
"May all the kings of the earth **praise you,** L*ORD,*
when they hear what you have decreed...." Psalm 138:4, emphasis added

WEEK 4

"Set me free from my prison,
that I may ***praise your name."*** Psalm 142:7a, emphasis added

WEEK 6

"Give thanks *to the* L*ORD, for he is good;*
his love endures forever." Psalm 106:1b, emphasis added
"Save us, L*ORD our God,*
and gather us from the nations,
that we may **give thanks** *to your holy name*
and glory in your praise." Psalm 106:47, emphasis added
"The L*ORD is my strength and my shield;*
my heart trusts in him, and he helps me.
My heart leaps for joy,
and with my song I praise him." Psalm 28:7
***"Praise the* LORD** *with the harp;*
make music to him on the ten-stringed lyre." Psalm 33:2, emphasis added

WEEK FOUR

PRAYERS OF LAMENT

PSALM 102

A prayer of an afflicted person who has grown weak and pours out a lament before the LORD.

1 Hear my prayer, LORD;
let my cry for help come to you.
2 Do not hide your face from me
when I am in distress.
Turn your ear to me;
when I call, answer me quickly.
3 For my days vanish like smoke;
my bones burn like glowing embers.
4 My heart is blighted and withered like grass;
I forget to eat my food.
5 In my distress I groan aloud
and am reduced to skin and bones.
6 I am like a desert owl,
like an owl among the ruins.
7 I lie awake; I have become
like a bird alone on a roof.
8 All day long my enemies taunt me;
those who rail against me use my name as a curse.
9 For I eat ashes as my food
and mingle my drink with tears
10 because of your great wrath,
for you have taken me up and thrown me aside.
11 My days are like the evening shadow;
I wither away like grass.
12 But you, LORD, sit enthroned forever;
your renown endures through all generations.
13 You will arise and have compassion on Zion,
for it is time to show favor to her;
the appointed time has come.
14 For her stones are dear to your servants;
her very dust moves them to pity.
15 The nations will fear the name of the LORD,
all the kings of the earth will revere your glory.
16 For the LORD will rebuild Zion
and appear in his glory.
17 He will respond to the prayer of the destitute;
he will not despise their plea.
18 Let this be written for a future generation,
that a people not yet created may praise the LORD:
19 "The LORD looked down from his sanctuary on high,
from heaven he viewed the earth,
20 to hear the groans of the prisoners
and release those condemned to death."
21 So the name of the LORD will be declared in Zion
and his praise in Jerusalem
22 when the peoples and the kingdoms
assemble to worship the LORD.
23 In the course of my life he broke my strength;
he cut short my days.
24 So I said:
"Do not take me away, my God, in the midst of my days;
your years go on through all generations.
25 In the beginning you laid the foundations of the earth,
and the heavens are the work of your hands.
26 They will perish, but you remain;
they will all wear out like a garment.
Like clothing you will change them
and they will be discarded.
27 But you remain the same,
and your years will never end.
28 The children of your servants will live in your presence;
their descendants will be established before you."

DAY 16

Hear My Cry

For the woman who needs to say she's not OK.

CLAIRE FOXX AND MELISSA SPOELSTRA

TODAY'S READING: Psalm 102

MAJOR MOMENT: One psalmist's despair stopped him from sleeping and eating, but it did not stop him from praying and trusting God.

KEY VERSE: Psalm 102:1
Hear my prayer, Lord; let my cry for help come to you.

"How are you?" asks the cashier scanning your bread.

"OK," you say, all the while thinking, *Trust me — you don't want to know.*

"That's good." She nods, polite but distracted.

"How are you?"

"Good."

"Good," you echo, searching for the meaning of the word. You want to cry. Or kick or scream or do anything but watch this stranger calmly bag your spaghetti as if you're not barely surviving the hardest week of your life.

Have you been here? When our hearts are broken and we're desperate for hope, we long for a safe place to pour out our pain, but often the world seems full of strangers.

That's why we need Psalm 102. This prayer reminds us we can tell God the truth when we're not OK. In fact, He *wants to know* — so we don't have to choose between praying honestly and praying faithfully to Him. We can choose to lament, which will be our prayer focus this week.

The person who penned this particular prayer began with a raw appeal to God to hear his cry. He entreated Yahweh not to hide His face but to turn His ear toward him (Psalm 102:2). Then he transitioned into a series of metaphors that emphasized the transitory and painful nature of life: smoke, embers and grass (Psalm 102:3-4). He didn't temper his complaints as he wrestled in the tension of what had meaning and what seemed meaningless.

> What is lament? How would you define it, and how does it make you feel?

A lament is more than a sad prayer. Pastor Matt Boga says to lament is to "tell God about your pain ... the good things lost, and the new pains found, but do so with a confident and eternal hope."[1]

> With this in mind, let's look at Psalm 102:3-11. Since God is all-knowing, no one can give Him new information. So why do you think the psalmist described his pain to God in excruciating detail?

NOTE FROM JOEL

The all-knowing aspect of God is theologically referred to as His omniscience. This word comes from Latin: *omni* meaning "all" and *scientia* meaning "knowledge." More specifically, this deals with God's perfect knowledge of Himself and all things He has created. Because God is the creator of all things, He thus knows all things.

This means there are no limits to God's knowledge. God knows everything present, (Psalm 33:13-15) past (Job 38:4-5) and future. (Psalm 139:4; Isaiah 46:10; Matthew 26:34) As a note of comfort, the implication is that God can never be caught off guard. He is not surprised by the events of the world. God is fully aware, and in His omniscience He is working all things together for the good of those who love Him and toward His ultimate glory. (Romans 8:28)

If you've ever wept in the arms of a friend on your worst day, you know these moments are about intimacy, not information. Because of who He is, weeping in God's arms has an exponentially greater effect: Lament doesn't reveal anything new to God, but it invites God to reveal Himself anew to us in our pain.

After reading Psalm 102, what would you say God revealed to the psalmist through his lament? Did this revelation change the *circumstances* of the psalmist's suffering or change his *perspective* on his suffering?

If you've ever felt like God wasn't answering your prayers because He didn't change your circumstances ... how does Psalm 102 offer a new way to look at these prayers?

Some scholars theorize that the writer of Psalm 102 was an Israelite who lived during the 70-year Babylonian exile God foretold through the prophet Jeremiah. Jeremiah described a burned-out landscape of ashes, fire and waste places (see Jeremiah 25) much like Psalm 102 depicts.

Yet what hopeful promise did God make to His exiled people in Jeremiah 23:3-4? How might this help us understand the hopeful shift in the psalmist's lament starting in Psalm 102:12 (*"But you, Lord …"*)?

In the end, what we know about Psalm 102 is that its writer suffered — but not without hope. Despair even stopped him from sleeping and eating, (vv. 4, 7) but it did not stop him from praying, which reminded him nothing can stop God.

PRAYER PRACTICE

God, when I look at my life today, I see withered grass and waste places. (Psalm 102:4-6) Sometimes my bones feel like they're burning inside me, but no one can see it. (v. 3) Honestly, I am not OK. I know I can't hide my pain from You — I want to tell You about it so You can reveal Yourself to me through it. You are "enthroned forever" and You endure "through all generations" (vv. 12, 24). Help me remember that all suffering has an end; only You are endless. In Jesus' name, amen.

[1] Why, LORD, do you stand far off?
Why do you hide yourself in times of trouble?
[2] In his arrogance the wicked man hunts down the weak,
who are caught in the schemes he devises.
[3] He boasts about the cravings of his heart;
he blesses the greedy and reviles the LORD.
[4] In his pride the wicked man does not seek him;
in all his thoughts there is no room for God.
[5] His ways are always prosperous;
your laws are rejected by him;
he sneers at all his enemies.
[6] He says to himself, "Nothing will ever shake me."
He swears, "No one will ever do me harm."
[7] His mouth is full of lies and threats;
trouble and evil are under his tongue.
[8] He lies in wait near the villages;
from ambush he murders the innocent.
His eyes watch in secret for his victims;
[9] like a lion in cover he lies in wait.
He lies in wait to catch the helpless;
he catches the helpless and drags them off in his net.
[10] His victims are crushed, they collapse;
they fall under his strength.
[11] He says to himself, "God will never notice;
he covers his face and never sees."
[12] Arise, LORD! Lift up your hand, O God.
Do not forget the helpless.
[13] Why does the wicked man revile God?
Why does he say to himself,
"He won't call me to account"?
[14] But you, God, see the trouble of the afflicted;
you consider their grief and take it in hand.
The victims commit themselves to you;
you are the helper of the fatherless.
[15] Break the arm of the wicked man;
call the evildoer to account for his wickedness
that would not otherwise be found out.
[16] The LORD is King for ever and ever;
the nations will perish from his land.
[17] You, LORD, hear the desire of the afflicted;
you encourage them, and you listen to their cry,
[18] defending the fatherless and the oppressed,
so that mere earthly mortals
will never again strike terror.

DAY 17

The Call of the Righteous

For the woman who doesn't know how to pray when it seems like evil is winning.

CLAIRE FOXX AND MELANIE DAVIS PORTER

TODAY'S READING: Psalm 10

MAJOR MOMENT: A psalmist wrestled with questions about God's hiddenness and the triumph of the wicked.

KEY VERSE: Psalm 10:1
Why, LORD, do you stand far off?
Why do you hide yourself in times of trouble?

It's hard to turn on the news without seeing the injustices innocent people suffer. We especially ache when offenders escape consequences, and frustration, anxiety and questions rise up as we witness the character and deeds of the ungodly. Something in our nature wants to see fairness be the rule of law for all (Proverbs 21:15).

The psalmist in today's reading was no different as he prayed for God's intervention. The call of the righteous psalmist both implored and trusted God to exact justice on those who plotted and carried out wickedness.

Psalm 10 begins with questions:

1. *"Why, LORD, do you* ________________ ____________ ____________ *?"* (v. 1a)
2. *"Why do you* ____________ ________________________ *in times of trouble?"* (v. 1b)

Sound familiar? Many of us have asked God some version of these questions when evil seems to be winning the battle for control of our lives and our world ... or maybe we've wanted to ask these questions but weren't sure we should. How could we accuse God of being unresponsive?

Well, let's look closer: Psalm 10 is not an accusatory prayer. It's a questioning one. Yes, the psalmist expresses confusion about why God seems distant from human suffering — but he also demonstrates faith.

Where we look for answers to our questions shows who we trust, and this psalmist trusted God, even when He didn't understand Him.

How do the psalmist's questions to God (vv. 1, 13) compare to the wicked man's *assumptions* about God in verses 4, 6 and 11?

What is the difference?

At times, the psalmist and the wicked man's observations about God are actually similar (for example: *"Why do you hide yourself"* in verse 1 and *"He covers his face and never sees"* in verse 11), but their heart postures are completely opposite. Assumptions come from pride in our own knowledge. Questions require humility: We have to admit we don't know. This is arguably the most vulnerable posture we can take in prayer — and that makes it perfect for lament.

What questions about justice and evil are troubling you today? Write them below.

In what ways might you pray to be a voice or vessel used by God for justice or against such evil?

In what ways can you respond to the everyday evils and injustice before you like the psalmist? Reflect on verse 14 and make a list below:

NOTE FROM JOEL

Theologically, these are referred to as questions of theodicy. The English word "theodicy" comes from two Greek words — *theos*, meaning "God," and *dikē*, meaning "justice" — which could be literally translated as "divine justice."[1] Rather than focusing on *why*, God assures us of *who*. We have limited knowledge, and our limits show up significantly when it comes to the problem of evil. A shift in perspective from why to who reorients our prayer to the perfect and present Triune God who is all-knowing and sufficient for all wrong to be restored.

When we've been devastated by evil schemes like Psalm 10 describes, it's painful to see the schemers go unpunished. We feel confused, even infuriated, which may tempt us to pray vengefully — like how Jesus' disciples once wanted to pray for *"fire [to come] down from heaven to destroy"* their offenders (Luke 9:54).

Read the whole story in Luke 9:51-56. How did Jesus respond?

Of course, this doesn't mean Jesus is uninterested in justice. What *"day"* does He mention in Matthew 12:36 and Matthew 10:15? What will happen on that day?

When we pray for God to *"call the evildoer to account"* (Psalm 10:15), we do so trusting that He will right every wrong — whether **today** or on **Judgment Day.** Moreover, we remember that we ourselves are wicked sinners who have benefitted from God's mercy.

According to theologian Thomas Hartwell Horne, the wicked person in Psalm 10 "wants no prophet to teach him, no priest to atone for him, no king to conduct for him; he needs neither a Christ to redeem, nor a Spirit to sanctify him; he believes no Providence, adores no Creator, and fears no Judge."[2]

Here's a hard question: Do you remember when this was true of you, before you knew Christ?

How might this shape your prayers about injustice? (Also see 2 Peter 3:9.)

Ultimately, God answered this psalmist's prayer not by resolving his questions about evil but by revealing His authority over evil. Make a short list of God's response as the psalmist recounts:

Similar to Psalm 10:17-18, Revelation 19:2 says God's judgments are "*true and just.*" That means God is just in every situation, even when our circumstances seem unfair to us. Whatever He decides to do is done without partiality toward rank, wealth or position. Because God is perfectly just and holy, He sets the standard to determine what is just. He can never be unjust.

PRAYER PRACTICE

Today, practice a breath prayer for one full minute. As you settle into prayer, close your eyes. With every inhale, repeat the words: Lord, I don't understand why.

And then exhale, repeating the words: But God, I trust in You.

A prayer of Moses the man of God.

1 Lord, you have been our dwelling place
throughout all generations.
2 Before the mountains were born
or you brought forth the whole world,
from everlasting to everlasting you are God.
3 You turn people back to dust,
saying, "Return to dust, you mortals."
4 A thousand years in your sight
are like a day that has just gone by,
or like a watch in the night.
5 Yet you sweep people away in the sleep of death—
they are like the new grass of the morning:
6 In the morning it springs up new,
but by evening it is dry and withered.
7 We are consumed by your anger
and terrified by your indignation.
8 You have set our iniquities before you,
our secret sins in the light of your presence.
9 All our days pass away under your wrath;
we finish our years with a moan.
10 Our days may come to seventy years,
or eighty, if our strength endures;
yet the best of them are but trouble and sorrow,
for they quickly pass, and we fly away.
11 If only we knew the power of your anger!
Your wrath is as great as the fear that is your due.
12 Teach us to number our days,
that we may gain a heart of wisdom.
13 Relent, LORD! How long will it be?
Have compassion on your servants.
14 Satisfy us in the morning with your unfailing love,
that we may sing for joy and be glad all our days.
15 Make us glad for as many days as you have afflicted us,
for as many years as we have seen trouble.
16 May your deeds be shown to your servants,
your splendor to their children.
17 May the favor of the Lord our God rest on us;
establish the work of our hands for us—
yes, establish the work of our hands.

DAY 18

A Prayer of Sorrow and Hope

For the woman who needs a way to grieve with hope.

CLAIRE FOXX AND CATHERINE MARTINEZ

TODAY'S READING: Psalm 90

MAJOR MOMENT: Moses lamented death but hoped for God's redemption.

KEY VERSE: Psalm 90:12
Teach us to number our days, that we may gain a heart of wisdom.

After the vivid descriptions of evil, sorrow and suffering we've read this week, the opening verses of Psalm 90, which praise God's eternal goodness and power, might not seem much like a lament. But by the time we get to verse 3, we see even these praises are mingled with pain, as God's eternality *"from everlasting to everlasting"* (v. 2) contrasts sharply with human mortality — from dust to dust. (v. 3)

Psalm 90 is a prayer of grief. In fact, theologian John Piper refers to it as a "death rehearsal."[1]

What do you think this means?

What phrases or ideas about death stand out to you in Psalm 90?

Psalm 90 is widely attributed to Moses, who led God's people from their exodus out of Egypt until their entrance to the promised land — including 40 years of wandering in the desert because they rebelled against God. This wandering may be reflected in the psalm's imagery: *"like a watch in the night,"* as Israelites would have done around the campfire (v. 4); grass that *"is dry and withered,"* as they would have seen in the desert (vv. 5-6); and days that *"pass away under your wrath"* (v. 9).[2]

Read Numbers 14:33-35. How does this help you understand what Moses may have been mourning in Psalm 90?

Moses was well-acquainted with grief, and his pain was much like what we face today. In Psalm 90:10 alone, he lamented two all-too-familiar sorrows:

1. Life always feels too short. Even if *"our days may come to seventy years, or eighty,"* they *"quickly pass, and we fly away."*
2. Life is full of hard work, challenges and problems (*"trouble and sorrow"*), which make our fleeting lives difficult.

Which of these sorrows is hardest for you to process today? Take a moment to tell God (or better yet, ask Him) why.

Death is certainly cause for lament. It's been the *cause* for lament since the garden of Eden. (Genesis 2:17) And none of us are born knowing how to process it: That's why Moses asked God to *"**Teach us** to number our days, that we may gain a heart of wisdom"* (Psalm 90:12, emphasis added).

Praying for wisdom is an easy "yes" — but it's hard to pray for that wisdom to be learned through a holy appreciation of our few and difficult, yet eternally valuable, days on earth. Moses prayed the hard prayer.

And so did Jesus. (Mark 14:36) Christ set the ultimate example for us by grieving His own impending death on the cross yet following God faithfully every day of His life:

- Jesus said, *"I am with you for only a short time"* (John 7:33). He lived less than half of what Moses said was a brief life. (Psalm 90:10) **But in 33 years, He changed the world by serving others in radical obedience to His Father.**
- Jesus' life was marked by sorrow, hardship and pain from the day He was born. (Matthew 2:13; Matthew 12:14; John 11:33-35) **But *"for the joy set before him he endured the cross"*** (Hebrews 12:2). **And then in His resurrection, He defeated death forever!**

In Psalm 90:15, what did Moses pray?

Because of Jesus, we know God has answered this prayer. In Christ, our eternal blessings will not only be *"as many"* (Psalm 90:15) as our present sufferings ... He promises *"an eternal glory that far outweighs them all"* (2 Corinthians 4:17).

PRAYER PRACTICE

Father God, thank You that You answer brokenhearted prayers. Please help me to remember this about You, especially when I feel devastated by how short and how difficult life seems. When my heart is crushed by grief for the ones I've lost and by fear of future losses, I dread numbering my days. But I trust You to teach me how to do this in a way that brings wisdom and eternal hope. (Psalm 90:12) Thank You for the opportunity to learn from You. In Jesus' name, amen.

If I Don't Feel Sad Right Now, *Do I Still Lament?*

Prayers of lament are not only a way to faithfully process life's hardest questions and emotions; they're also a kind of spiritual discipline. Lament is as much a part of following Jesus as confession or thanksgiving — though we don't often encourage one another to lament in the same way we encourage accountability or gratitude.

Of course, Scripture tells us to *"rejoice in the Lord"* (Philippians 4:4) because we have so much to celebrate in Christ! But here on earth, there is also much to grieve, and it's good to remember that for several reasons:

ONE

Lament prepares us for future sorrow.

"There is a time for everything, and a season for every activity under the heavens: a time to be born and a time to die,

... a time to weep and a time to laugh, a time to mourn and a time to dance ..." (Ecclesiastes 3:1-2, 4)

If we think of lament as a "last resort" prayer, to be prayed only during the hardest moments of life, we can start to think of hardship itself as exceptional, something we can hopefully avoid if we live well and pray the "right" prayers the rest of the time. Yet Jesus Himself tells us, *"In this world you will have trouble."* Lament teaches us to expect these troubles — but not to fear them, for Christ has *"overcome the world"* (John 16:33).

TWO

Lament prompts us toward compassion.

"Rejoice with those who rejoice; mourn with those who mourn." (Romans 12:15)

We don't lament just for ourselves; we lament for others who are suffering even when we aren't. When we're in a great mood, the last thing we may want to do is pray for our newly widowed neighbor, our co-worker struggling with depression, or people affected by natural disasters in a nation thousands of miles away ... but the ministry of our prayers is eternal. After all, the command to *"mourn with those who mourn"* in Romans 12:15 follows the command to *"bless those who persecute you"* (v. 14) — not because either is easy but because both are holy.

THREE

Lament pivots our perspective toward eternity.

"But woe to you who are rich, for you have already received your comfort. Woe to you who are well fed now, for you will go hungry. Woe to you who laugh now, for you will mourn and weep." (Luke 6:24-25)

Sometimes we don't "feel like" lamenting because we're a bit too comfortable with life in this world — which is only temporary. Even our joy on earth is not meant to distract us from the reality that creation is *"groaning ... and not only the creation, but we ourselves"* while we await Jesus' return (Romans 8:22-23, ESV). As we lament that the world is horribly broken, we also anticipate the end of all lament, when Christ will redeem His creation forever just as He has promised! (Revelation 21:4)

For the director of music. To the tune of "The Doe of the Morning." A psalm of David.

1 My God, my God, why have you forsaken me?
Why are you so far from saving me,
so far from my cries of anguish?
2 My God, I cry out by day, but you do not answer,
by night, but I find no rest.
3 Yet you are enthroned as the Holy One;
you are the one Israel praises.
4 In you our ancestors put their trust;
they trusted and you delivered them.
5 To you they cried out and were saved;
in you they trusted and were not put to shame.
6 But I am a worm and not a man,
scorned by everyone, despised by the people.
7 All who see me mock me;
they hurl insults, shaking their heads.
8 "He trusts in the LORD," they say,
"let the LORD rescue him.
Let him deliver him,
since he delights in him."
9 Yet you brought me out of the womb;
you made me trust in you, even at my mother's breast.
10 From birth I was cast on you;
from my mother's womb you have been my God.
11 Do not be far from me,
for trouble is near
and there is no one to help.
12 Many bulls surround me;
strong bulls of Bashan encircle me.
13 Roaring lions that tear their prey
open their mouths wide against me.
14 I am poured out like water,
and all my bones are out of joint.
My heart has turned to wax;
it has melted within me.
15 My mouth is dried up like a potsherd,
and my tongue sticks to the roof of my mouth;
you lay me in the dust of death.

16 Dogs surround me,
a pack of villains encircles me;
they pierce my hands and my feet.
17 All my bones are on display;
people stare and gloat over me.
18 They divide my clothes among them
and cast lots for my garment.
19 But you, LORD, do not be far from me.
You are my strength; come quickly to help me.
20 Deliver me from the sword,
my precious life from the power of the dogs.
21 Rescue me from the mouth of the lions;
save me from the horns of the wild oxen.
22 I will declare your name to my people;
in the assembly I will praise you.
23 You who fear the LORD, praise him!
All you descendants of Jacob, honor him!
Revere him, all you descendants of Israel!
24 For he has not despised or scorned
the suffering of the afflicted one;
he has not hidden his face from him
but has listened to his cry for help.
25 From you comes the theme of my praise in the great assembly;
before those who fear you I will fulfill my vows.
26 The poor will eat and be satisfied;
those who seek the LORD will praise him—
may your hearts live forever!
27 All the ends of the earth
will remember and turn to the LORD,
and all the families of the nations
will bow down before him,
28 for dominion belongs to the LORD
and he rules over the nations.
29 All the rich of the earth will feast and worship;
all who go down to the dust will kneel before him—
those who cannot keep themselves alive.
30 Posterity will serve him;
future generations will be told about the Lord.
31 They will proclaim his righteousness,
declaring to a people yet unborn:
He has done it!

DAY 19

Is Anybody There?

For the woman who needs to know she's not alone.

CLAIRE FOXX AND KAREN EHMAN

TODAY'S READING: Psalm 22

MAJOR MOMENT: David's suffering prophesied Jesus' redemptive suffering on the cross.

KEY VERSE: Psalm 22:19
But you, Lord, do not be far from me.
You are my strength; come quickly to help me.

Do you have a favorite worship song? Maybe it's an old spiritual your grandma used to hum while folding laundry, a hymn that gives you chills, or a new praise song on the radio that offers much-needed hope. What probably doesn't come to mind is Psalm 22.

Not quite "Amazing Grace," is it?

That's why it's fascinating that Psalm 22 includes instructions "to the choirmaster," suggesting psalms like this one may have been sung or recited by soloists in temple assemblies.[1] This approach seems to suit Psalm 22 — one man's lonely lament. But importantly, the psalm itself also draws attention to *"the great assembly"* of God's people (v. 25), describing the psalmist, David, as singing *"in the assembly"* (v. 22).

How does this image of God's people surrounding the lonely psalmist change your perspective on his prayer of affliction in verses 1-18?

How does this change your perspective on *your* affliction and *your* prayers?

In verse 16, David groaned, *"a pack of villains encircles me."* But as David prayed, God reminded him that he was part of a greater company: a Kingdom of faithful fellow sufferers *"those who seek the LORD will praise him"* (v. 26). As Christian therapist and author K.J. Ramsey says, lament "guide[s] our whole selves to participate in ... the gospel story of interdependence."[2] And there's perhaps no better example of this than Psalm 22, as David's suffering drew him near not only to God's people but to God's own Son.

Complete the chart below to highlight a few of many ways Psalm 22 prophesied Jesus' suffering on the cross:

GOSPEL ACCOUNTS OF JESUS' CRUCIFIXION	PROPHECY IN PSALM 22
Matthew 27:39-43	
John 19:23-24	
Mark 15:34	
Matthew 27:46	

The gospel changes everything! This includes our prayers of lament. Because he hoped in Jesus, the most alone David ever felt was actually the least alone he'd ever been. On earth, his clearest view of heaven was seen through tear-filled eyes. And the same is true for us: When we cry out, *"My God, my God, why have you forsaken me?"* (Psalm 22:1; Matthew 27:46; Mark 15:34), we speak the very words of Jesus Christ — who is our Savior and Immanuel, **God with us.** (Matthew 1:23)

NOTE FROM JOEL

As we look to the cross, it is good for us to pause and consider the depth of loneliness Jesus felt as He not only endured the physical pain of the cross but absorbed the spiritual pain of sin in atonement for humanity. Jesus always enjoyed and experienced the presence of the Father and the empowerment of the Spirit. Yet on one day in His human existence, He experienced utter loneliness.

In Matthew 27:46, Jesus cried out not in triumph but in agony. Jesus was abandoned by His disciples, (Matthew 26:56) rejected and denied, (Matthew 26:69-75) and the religious rulers and Israelites all turned on Him (Matthew 26:57-68) as the Romans tormented Him (Matthew 27:27-31).[3] Yet this darkest day of human history brought about the victory of Jesus so you and I would *never* have to be alone ever again.

According to Isaiah 53:4, whose grief did Jesus bear? Whose sorrows did He carry?

Friend, Jesus suffered for you, and He suffers with you. You are never alone. In Christ, we weep together and hope together on our hardest days, declaring that our worship does not come from our circumstances or even our feelings: *"From you [God] comes [our] praise in the great assembly"* (Psalm 22:25).

PRAYER PRACTICE

Write a prayer of confession and need. End your prayer in an acknowledgement and proclamation of who you know Jesus to be.

A maskil of David. When he was in the cave.
A prayer.

1 I cry aloud to the LORD;
  I lift up my voice to the LORD for mercy.
2 I pour out before him my complaint;
  before him I tell my trouble.

3 When my spirit grows faint within me,
  it is you who watch over my way.
In the path where I walk
  people have hidden a snare for me.
4 Look and see, there is no one at my right hand;
  no one is concerned for me.
I have no refuge;
  no one cares for my life.

5 I cry to you, LORD;
  I say, "You are my refuge,
  my portion in the land of the living."

6 Listen to my cry,
  for I am in desperate need;
rescue me from those who pursue me,
  for they are too strong for me.
7 Set me free from my prison,
  that I may praise your name.
Then the righteous will gather about me
  because of your goodness to me.

DAY 20

From Prison to Praise

For the woman who is desperate for a safe place.

CLAIRE FOXX AND MEI AU

TODAY'S READING: Psalm 142

MAJOR MOMENT: When hiding from his enemies, David's true refuge was God.

KEY VERSE: Psalm 142:7

Set me free from my prison, that I may praise your name.
Then the righteous will gather about me because of your goodness to me.

To wrap up our week, let's look at one last psalm: Psalm 142, another lament of David. Read the psalm below, along with the notes and questions we've included alongside it, and consider how it relates to what we've studied this week. Add your own notes, underlining and highlighting as the Lord teaches you through this prayer.

PSALM 142	**NOTES**
A maskil of David. When he was in the cave. A prayer.	See 1 Samuel 22:1 and 1 Samuel 24:1-3, two passages that describe when David was in a cave.
1 I cry aloud to the LORD; I lift up my voice to the LORD for mercy. 2 I pour out before him my complaint; before him I tell my trouble.	**Complaint before** God is not the same as **complaint against** God. For example, compare David's complaint here to the Israelites' ungrateful grumblings in Numbers 14 (and look at how God responded very differently!).
3 When my spirit grows faint within me, it is you who watch over my way. In the path where I walk people have hidden a snare for me. 4 Look and see, there is no one at my right hand; no one is concerned for me.	David doesn't name those who are causing him pain in this psalm. This makes it easy for us to pray these words to God about our own life situations (whoever "they" may be for us) — and it also highlights the importance of the only name that does appear in Psalm 142: God's name.

I have no refuge;
no one cares for my life.

5 I cry to you, LORD;
I say, "You are my refuge,
my portion in the land of the living."

6 Listen to my cry,
for I am in desperate need;
rescue me from those who pursue me,
for they are too strong for me.
7 Set me free from my prison,
that I may praise your name.
Then the righteous will gather about me
because of your goodness to me.

Underline the uses of God's covenant name, *LORD*, in Psalm 142.

What a contrast: prison vs. refuge. A prison protects those outside from those inside, but a place of refuge does the opposite. What other differences do you see between these two places, and what might this tell you about God?

The Hebrew word *tiḡ-mōl,* translated ***"you will deal bountifully,"*** (ESV, emphasis added) is similar to the word *way-yiḡ-mōl* used in Numbers 17:8 to describe Aaron's wooden staff miraculously bearing almonds. Could this image of dead wood becoming fruitful by God's power relate to David's prayer for God to redeem his suffering?

REFLECTION PROMPTS

What truths from this week's study is God reinforcing as you read Psalm 142?

What new truths about prayer in suffering is God revealing to you in Psalm 142? (Flip back to Day 16: Has your definition of "lament" changed? How?)

Think of a time God brought you out of a season of grief, isolation or despair. How did He reveal His goodness to you?

PRAYER PRACTICE

Whether you need God to be your refuge in your current suffering, prepare your heart for future suffering, or soften your heart toward the suffering of others, write your own prayer below using Psalm 142 as inspiration.

WEEK FOUR

WEEKEND REFLECTION

Sometimes it feels overwhelming to talk to God about the most excruciating parts of our lives. The ones that pierce us so deeply it's hard to talk about them at all because just saying the person's name ... the diagnosis ... the date of the accident ... feels like another trauma. The ones that leave us so confused and angry we consider them unmentionable or even unthinkable. But hopefully it's been comforting to see that the psalmists withheld none of their complicated feelings in their prayers; when their bones were burning (Psalm 102:3) or their hearts were melting, (Psalm 22:14) they said so. But they also praised the kindness, nearness and sovereignty of a trustworthy God who will *"satisfy us in the morning with [His] unfailing love"* (Psalm 90:14) even on our worst days.

Every bit as undeniable as the pain in these prayers is the presence of God with those who prayed them. And that same God is with us today. He is with you right now. He hears your heart's cry. He mourns alongside you as sin and death ravage this world — the world where His Son suffered and died as a *"man of suffering"* (Isaiah 53:3) — a world He has destined for eternal redemption because Jesus' grave, the ultimate pit of suffering, is now and forever empty! The psalms of lament in His Word are an example, a kindness and a gift to you, a guide for processing the crises of this life as "reasons for God's coming, not tokens of His distance."[1]

So even if you're not OK ...
Even if you have questions ...
Even if you're grieving ...
Even if you feel alone ...
Even if you're desperate for safety ...

Let's pray.

A PRAYER FOR YOU

Lord, when we're suffering, it feels like our energy is consumed by problems we can't solve, pain we can't escape, and people we can't save. But we want to be near You in every moment, even the most painful ones. Especially the most painful ones. So please show us Your grace toward messy, vulnerable, humbly question-filled prayers. By the power of Your Holy Spirit, help us to pray more often and more desperately so we can experience more of You. Please show us how to grieve together and grieve with hope. Remind us that we suffer not because You fail to protect us or because Your plans are thwarted by the enemy; "we share in his sufferings in order that we may also share in his glory" (Romans 8:17). The enemy is fighting a losing battle. You are victorious, and You are redeeming it all. In Jesus' name, amen.

WEEK FIVE

PRAYERS OF SUPPLICATION

Of David.

1 Do not fret because of those who are evil
or be envious of those who do wrong;
2 for like the grass they will soon wither,
like green plants they will soon die away.
3 Trust in the LORD and do good;
dwell in the land and enjoy safe pasture.
4 Take delight in the LORD,
and he will give you the desires of your heart.
5 Commit your way to the LORD;
trust in him and he will do this:
6 He will make your righteous reward shine like the dawn,
your vindication like the noonday sun.
7 Be still before the LORD
and wait patiently for him;
do not fret when people succeed in their ways,
when they carry out their wicked schemes.
8 Refrain from anger and turn from wrath;
do not fret—it leads only to evil.
9 For those who are evil will be destroyed,
but those who hope in the LORD will inherit the land.
10 A little while, and the wicked will be no more;
though you look for them, they will not be found.
11 But the meek will inherit the land
and enjoy peace and prosperity.
12 The wicked plot against the righteous
and gnash their teeth at them;
13 but the Lord laughs at the wicked,
for he knows their day is coming.
14 The wicked draw the sword
and bend the bow
to bring down the poor and needy,
to slay those whose ways are upright.
15 But their swords will pierce their own hearts,
and their bows will be broken.
16 Better the little that the righteous have
than the wealth of many wicked;
17 for the power of the wicked will be broken,
but the LORD upholds the righteous.
18 The blameless spend their days under the LORD's care,
and their inheritance will endure forever.
19 In times of disaster they will not wither;
in days of famine they will enjoy plenty.
20 But the wicked will perish:
Though the LORD's enemies are like the flowers of the field,
they will be consumed, they will go up in smoke.
21 The wicked borrow and do not repay,
but the righteous give generously;
22 those the LORD blesses will inherit the land,
but those he curses will be destroyed.

23 The LORD makes firm the steps
of the one who delights in him;
24 though he may stumble, he will not fall,
for the LORD upholds him with his hand.
25 I was young and now I am old,
yet I have never seen the righteous forsaken
or their children begging bread.
26 They are always generous and lend freely;
their children will be a blessing.
27 Turn from evil and do good;
then you will dwell in the land forever.
28 For the LORD loves the just
and will not forsake his faithful ones.
Wrongdoers will be completely destroyed;
the offspring of the wicked will perish.
29 The righteous will inherit the land
and dwell in it forever.
30 The mouths of the righteous utter wisdom,
and their tongues speak what is just.
31 The law of their God is in their hearts;
their feet do not slip.
32 The wicked lie in wait for the righteous,
intent on putting them to death;
33 but the LORD will not leave them in the power of the wicked
or let them be condemned when brought to trial.
34 Hope in the LORD
and keep his way.
He will exalt you to inherit the land;
when the wicked are destroyed, you will see it.
35 I have seen a wicked and ruthless man
flourishing like a luxuriant native tree,
36 but he soon passed away and was no more;
though I looked for him, he could not be found.
37 Consider the blameless, observe the upright;
a future awaits those who seek peace.
38 But all sinners will be destroyed;
there will be no future for the wicked.
39 The salvation of the righteous comes from the LORD;
he is their stronghold in time of trouble.
40 The LORD helps them and delivers them;
he delivers them from the wicked and saves them,
because they take refuge in him.

DAY 21

Leaving Our Burdens in God's Hands

For the woman who needs to be reminded she can talk to God about anything.

SHAE HILL AND MARISSA HENLEY

TODAY'S READING: Psalm 37

MAJOR MOMENT: David prayed for a heart that would delight in the Lord.

KEY VERSES: Psalm 37:5-6

Commit your way to the LORD; trust in him and he will do this: He will make your righteous reward shine like the dawn, your vindication like the noonday sun.

This week we will be focusing on prayers of supplication. Supplication can be defined as the action of asking or begging for something earnestly or humbly. This category of prayer may be the one we're most familiar with, but it may also birth the most tension and angst for us as believers.

Why? Asking God for things we desire, big or small, requires deep trust in Him. We surrender to Him the potential outcomes of those prayers: the timing of His answer ... the delivery ... or if they'll be answered at all.

When the ancient Israelites sang Psalm 37 in worship, they learned how to bring their requests to God and trust Him with every anxiety-provoking situation they faced.

How do these words both encourage and challenge you in praying for things you want or need?

NOTE FROM JOEL

In the opening line of verse 3, the Hebrew words hold significant meaning: *"Trust [bā·ṭăḥ] in the* L*ORD [yhwh]* . . . ." The Hebrew word *bā·ṭăḥ* has to do with placing our confidence in someone. It implies reliance. And *yhwh* is the intimate Hebrew name of God; it was uniquely given to the Israelites as evidence of their special relationship with God. In fact, it was common when reading Scripture out loud that, as a sign of respect, the Israelites would not even say the name *yhwh* out loud. When I was learning Hebrew, my professor did something similar: When my classmates and I read Scripture out loud and we came across the name *yhwh*, he would have us substitute *adonai* (meaning "Lord").

This information is important because it lets us in on the special way God relates to His people. He wants to be known and proves Himself trustworthy. One way is through the revelation of His own special name to His people in the Old Testament. And today, we have something even greater in significance — the Word that became flesh: Jesus. (John 1:14) If we want to be reminded of the trustworthy character of God, we simply need to look at Jesus.

Psalm 37:4 is probably one of the most commonly quoted verses in conversation about prayer. It's also one of the most misunderstood and misapplied verses.

Write Psalm 37:4 below.

It's so easy to zone in on *"he will give you the desires of your heart"* and neglect the first part: *"Take delight in the LORD."* As we posture our hearts to talk to God in prayer, it's crucial for us to remember that prayer isn't a transactional process that exists only for us to get what we want. Prayer is an open door of communication so we can draw near to God, delight in Him and commune with Him, knowing confidently that He hears our every word.

Can we come to God with anything on our hearts, including our desires, wishes, hopes and dreams? Absolutely. But, friend, prayer is so much more than that. Think about it like this: If you had a friend you *only* talked to when you needed a favor, wouldn't your relationship begin to feel transactional?

Is there a time in your life where it was tempting for prayer to become overly transactional? How did this affect your relationship with God and your trust in Him?

Psalm 37 mentions dwelling in or inheriting the land six times (Psalm 37:3; Psalm 37:9; Psalm 37:11; Psalm 37:22; Psalm 37:29; Psalm 37:34). For 21st-century Christians, this may seem like a strange theme in a psalm about trusting the Lord, but for the ancient Israelites, the promised land of Canaan was a symbol of God's covenant promises to them and of the inheritance for His people.

When David wrote that *"the righteous will inherit the land and dwell in it forever"* (Psalm 37:29), he wasn't saying that good things always happen to good people or that Israel would earn the promised land by being righteous. The land was God's gracious gift to them. It was the inheritance He promised to those who received His covenant and were made righteous by faith (Genesis 17:1-8; Romans 9:30-32).

Their physical inheritance foreshadowed the spiritual inheritance received by those who trust in Christ. First Peter 1:3-5 says that those who have been born again by God's mercy have a living hope and heavenly inheritance. This inheritance was secured through the life, death and resurrection of Jesus Christ and is given to all who trust in Him. God's gracious gifts to us include redemption through Christ's blood, forgiveness of our sins, adoption as His children, guidance from His Holy Spirit, and assurance of an eternal home with Him in glory (Ephesians 1:3-14).

Pause for a few moments and really consider what you think of as your inheritance in Christ Jesus. How would you characterize the 'land' you are inheriting and will occupy or dwell in? What is the enemy or evil you are needing the Lord to give you victory over?

Do not think first *of the* desires of thy heart, but think first *of* delighting thyself in thy God. If thou hast accepted him *as* thy Lord, he is thine; so delight in him, *and then* he will give thee the desires *of* thy heart.

CHARLES SPURGEON[1]

It's not just about the prayers we're praying. The posture we're praying in is of equal importance ... a posture of humility, trust, and patience.

> Look at verses 7, 18-19, 23-24 and 34 in Psalm 37. Write down any words that stand out to you regarding the posture of prayer you want to maintain in your heart.

As you continue on this 30-day prayer journey, remember the words you've discovered in Psalm 37 and the posture of prayer you want to walk in.

Finally, receive the prayer written for you below. Declare these words aloud as your prayer practice today and remember that God hears every supplication you pour out to Him.

PRAYER PRACTICE

Heavenly Father, You know my every need. I know when I draw close to You in prayer, You hear me. Oh, Lord, it's so hard to trust You completely with things I want or worry about in current circumstances ... relationally, financially, emotionally, mentally, physically, spiritually. Remind me of the words of Psalm 37:7. I pray that I would be still before You and wait patiently for You through every single item on my prayer list. I trust You with the things most precious to me. I trust You with the unknowns in my future. I trust You with the things that stir up the most anxiety inside me. I trust You, Lord. Help me walk out this trust faithfully. In Jesus' name, amen.

A Prayer of David.

1 Hear me, LORD, my plea is just;
listen to my cry.
Hear my prayer—
it does not rise from deceitful lips.
2 Let my vindication come from you;
may your eyes see what is right.
3 Though you probe my heart,
though you examine me at night and test me,
you will find that I have planned no evil;
my mouth has not transgressed.
4 Though people tried to bribe me,
I have kept myself from the ways of the violent
through what your lips have commanded.
5 My steps have held to your paths;
my feet have not stumbled.
6 I call on you, my God, for you will answer me;
turn your ear to me and hear my prayer.
7 Show me the wonders of your great love,
you who save by your right hand
those who take refuge in you from their foes.
8 Keep me as the apple of your eye;
hide me in the shadow of your wings
9 from the wicked who are out to destroy me,
from my mortal enemies who surround me.
10 They close up their callous hearts,
and their mouths speak with arrogance.
11 They have tracked me down, they now surround me,
with eyes alert, to throw me to the ground.
12 They are like a lion hungry for prey,
like a fierce lion crouching in cover.
13 Rise up, LORD, confront them, bring them down;
with your sword rescue me from the wicked.
14 By your hand save me from such people, LORD,
from those of this world whose reward is in this life.
May what you have stored up for the wicked fill their bellies;
may their children gorge themselves on it,
and may there be leftovers for their little ones.
15 As for me, I will be vindicated and will see your face;
when I awake, I will be satisfied with seeing your likeness.

DAY 22

Praying Through the Hard Places

For the woman who longs to be delivered out of the hardship she's facing.

SHAE HILL AND DENISE PASS

TODAY'S READING: Psalm 17

MAJOR MOMENT: David cried out to God in times of crisis, asking to be delivered from trouble and enemy persecution.

KEY VERSE: Psalm 17:6

I call on you, my God, for you will answer me;
turn your ear to me and hear my prayer.

The entire book of Psalms lends itself to prayer, but there aren't many psalms explicitly called "a prayer." Psalm 17 is one: It's titled "A Prayer of David." While we don't know exactly when David prayed these words, we can confidently say it was during a time of crisis.

In verse 1, David believed the cause he was bringing to the Lord was *"just"* and that his cries to the Lord were not spoken *"from deceitful lips."* This goes back to what we learned about confession and God's forgiveness during Week 2 of this study and what we said yesterday about the posture of our hearts when we enter prayer. Look at what David says in Psalm 17:3: *"Though you probe my heart, though you examine me at night and test me, you will find that I have planned no evil; my mouth has not transgressed."*

> Go to Psalm 139:23-24, also a psalm of David. Notice David's posture toward the Lord and the humility he prays in. How might you invite the Lord to search your heart and thoughts like David as you bring Him your requests?

David invited God to test his heart; therefore, he knew he could enter a time of prayer with the confidence of a clean heart — not because he was perfect but because God's forgiveness is. Commentator James Boice says "open and unconfessed sin is a great prayer barrier. An upright life is a strong basis for appeals."[1] Boice also suggests the following questions for examining our hearts before we pray:

Am I being disobedient?
Am I being selfish?
Am I neglecting some important duty?
Is there a wrong I should first make right?
Are my priorities in order?

In keeping his heart swept clean, David was careful to not cross over into sin in the way he prayed about his crisis or his enemies.

Look up Genesis 4:7. What does this verse instruct us to do in regard to sin?

Even though David was in crisis, he didn't take matters into his own hands. *"Let my vindication come from you; may your eyes see what is right."* (Psalm 17:2) David wanted the Lord to hear his cry, (v. 1) answer his words, (v. 6) protect him from what he was facing, (vv. 8-9) and deliver his soul from the wicked around him, (vv. 13-14) but he refused to take charge of these things *himself.*

This reveals David's deep trust in God. David very much believed that, at any moment, God could rescue him out of the troubling situations he was in — and he wanted to be delivered. But he trusted God to be the Deliverer.

Isn't this easier said than done? Especially when you're right in the middle of hard circumstances, feeling misunderstood, misrepresented or mistreated by others?

David understood this too.

Read Psalm 17:10-15. What was David saying about his enemies?

Look up Philippians 3:18-20 and jot down any similarities you notice.

AM I BEING DISOBEDIENT?

AM I BEING SELFISH?

EXAMINING MY HEART BEFORE I PRAY

AM I NEGLECTING SOME IMPORTANT DUTY?

IS THERE A WRONG I SHOULD FIRST MAKE RIGHT?

ARE MY PRIORITIES IN ORDER?

In conclusion, David reminds us of four important things to remember about prayer, especially when we're walking through difficult circumstances:

Four Things to Remember About Prayer

1. We can bring our honest, unfiltered thoughts to God in prayer without crossing over into sin. (Psalm 17:1)

2. What we're experiencing may not feel like love, but it does not change God's unfailing love toward us. (Psalm 17:7)

3. God will continue to protect us even in times of crisis or trouble. (Psalm 17:8)

4. Hard and heartbreaking times don't have to prevent us from seeing and meeting with God. (Psalm 17:15)

When we cry out to God in supplication, we know God sees and hears us too. We also know that our Savior understands. Jesus offered prayers of supplication while on earth; for instance, the Lord's Prayer includes supplication for *"our daily bread"* (Matthew 6:11). In the prayers and teachings of Christ, we see that God's heart is for His people to bring their needs to Him. *"If you, then, though you are evil, know how to give good gifts to your children, how much more will your Father in heaven give good gifts to those who ask him!"* (Matthew 7:11).

PRAYER PRACTICE

Borrow these words from David and declare them as a prayer over yourself, your family and any circumstances you're facing right now:

"I call on you, my God, for you will answer me; turn your ear to me and hear my prayer. Show me the wonders of your great love, you who save by your right hand those who take refuge in you from their foes. Keep me as the apple of your eye; hide me in the shadow of your wings." (Psalm 17:6–8)

A psalm of David.

1 LORD, hear my prayer,
listen to my cry for mercy;
in your faithfulness and righteousness
come to my relief.
2 Do not bring your servant into judgment,
for no one living is righteous before you.
3 The enemy pursues me,
he crushes me to the ground;
he makes me dwell in the darkness
like those long dead.
4 So my spirit grows faint within me;
my heart within me is dismayed.
5 I remember the days of long ago;
I meditate on all your works
and consider what your hands have done.
6 I spread out my hands to you;
I thirst for you like a parched land.
7 Answer me quickly, LORD;
my spirit fails.
Do not hide your face from me
or I will be like those who go down to the pit.
8 Let the morning bring me word of your unfailing love,
for I have put my trust in you.
Show me the way I should go,
for to you I entrust my life.
9 Rescue me from my enemies, LORD,
for I hide myself in you.
10 Teach me to do your will,
for you are my God;
may your good Spirit
lead me on level ground.
11 For your name's sake, LORD, preserve my life;
in your righteousness, bring me out of trouble.
12 In your unfailing love, silence my enemies;
destroy all my foes,
for I am your servant.

DAY 23

Hesed and Prayer

For the woman who is asking God, What's next? Where do I go from here?

SHAE HILL AND KELLYE SCHIFFNER CARVER

TODAY'S READING: Psalm 143

MAJOR MOMENT: David prayed for God to direct his life and decisions.

KEY VERSE: Psalm 143:8

Let the morning bring me word of your unfailing love, for I have put my trust in you.
Show me the way I should go, for to you I entrust my life.

Psalm 143 is yet another prayer where David is crying out to God in a time of crisis. Again we see that the psalms are not cookie-cutter prayers written by perfect people in perfect circumstances. The psalms contain real words cried out by real people, sometimes in real hardship.

Does this realness bring you hope and comfort? Why or why not?

In what ways?

May we be reminded today to dig into real, honest prayers to God. We don't have to like what we're facing — even Jesus asked God to change the plan. (Mark 14:36) But like David, may we not allow what we're going through to dry up our thirst and desire for closeness with God. (Psalm 143:6)

In Psalm 143:1 David says, "*Lord, hear my prayer, listen to my cry for mercy; in your faithfulness and righteousness come to my relief.*" Here, we see David desperately seeking God's attention while calling on His faithfulness and righteousness. In verse 2, he asked the Lord to deal with him not according to what he deserved (because of sin) but according to the Lord's mercy. Whatever David was walking through, he knew he would be lost without direction from God. He didn't try to manipulate God but simply prayed for God to act according to His character.

Is there a situation where you're asking God for direction right now? What have your prayers about this situation sounded like up until now?

Beginning in Psalm 143:5, David teaches us something so important about how to walk through hard times: He said, *"I remember ..."* In all he was processing, David paused to remember God's works and goodness from the past.

Why is remembering important? Because we so easily forget, especially when something currently doesn't feel good or God feels silent. When we're going through times of difficulty, those are the exact moments we should call our souls to *"forget not"* (Psalm 103:2), reminding our forgetful hearts that God has not forgotten us. The great theologian Charles Spurgeon describes it this way: "When we see nothing new which can cheer us, let us think upon old things. We once had merry days, days of deliverance, and joy and thanksgiving; why not again?"[1]

Take a moment to journal about God's goodness and faithfulness you've experienced in the past. How does remembering the past inform your current doubt or uncertainties about the future?

Depending on your translation, your Bible might speak of God's *"unfailing love," "steadfast love"* (ESV) or *"faithfulness"* (NASB) in Psalm 143:8. The Hebrew word here is hesed, which occurs almost 250 times in the Bible. It means kindness, mercy or affection, especially toward the lowly or needy. In regard to God, hesed is often translated as "lovingkindness," an abundant, extensive, everlasting goodness and kindness. While difficult to translate directly to English, this concept also evokes words like "mercy" or "fidelity." It further involves redemption, protection and covenant keeping. In fact, when God described Himself, steadfast love comprised a critical piece of His identity (Exodus 34:6-7).

David didn't just need the *"unfailing love"* of God (Psalm 143:8a); He also needed the guidance of God.

Let's look at Psalm 143:8b: *"Show me the* ________________ *I should* ________________, *for to you I entrust my life."*

In verse 10, David continues to pray: "*Teach me to do your will, for you are my God; may your good Spirit lead me on level ground.*"

Let's dig deeper into three parts of supplication found in these verses:

SHOW ME

Verse 8

David didn't want to miss what God was doing or where God was leading. He said *"show me the way,"* or *"make me know the way"* (ESV). David asked for God to reveal Himself and for his own soul to remain attentive.

TEACH ME

Verse 10

David knew he needed God's instruction; he had the humility to ask God to teach him to do God's will.

LEAD ME

Verse 10

Moving forward, David prayed for God's *"good Spirit"* to lead him. He knew how prone he was, like all of us are, to go his own way. He didn't want to assume he knew where to go or what the right next step was. He needed God's leadership.

With this in mind, we can follow David's example of approaching God with our requests, knowing He will continue to shower us with *hesed* today:

- We can request God's presence and quick response (Psalm 143:7).
- We can ask for reassurance of God's hesed and affirm our trust in Him (Psalm 143:8).
- We can lift up our souls to the Lord and ask for direction (Psalm 143:8).
- We can request rescue and hide ourselves in God (Psalm 143:9).
- We can ask God to teach and lead us (Psalm 143:10).
- We can plead for protection and escape from trouble (Psalm 143:11).
- We can hope in God's power to silence and defeat our enemies out of His hesed (Psalm 143:12).

PRAYER PRACTICE

To close today, write your own prayer about a situation where you need God's direction. Incorporate these three phrases in your prayer:

Show me …

Teach me …

Lead me …

For the director of music. A psalm of David.

1 In you, LORD, I have taken refuge;
let me never be put to shame;
deliver me in your righteousness.
2 Turn your ear to me,
come quickly to my rescue;
be my rock of refuge,
a strong fortress to save me.
3 Since you are my rock and my fortress,
for the sake of your name lead and guide me.
4 Keep me free from the trap that is set for me,
for you are my refuge.
5 Into your hands I commit my spirit;
deliver me, LORD, my faithful God.
6 I hate those who cling to worthless idols;
as for me, I trust in the LORD.
7 I will be glad and rejoice in your love,
for you saw my affliction
and knew the anguish of my soul.
8 You have not given me into the hands of the enemy
but have set my feet in a spacious place.
9 Be merciful to me, LORD, for I am in distress;
my eyes grow weak with sorrow,
my soul and body with grief.
10 My life is consumed by anguish
and my years by groaning;
my strength fails because of my affliction,
and my bones grow weak.
11 Because of all my enemies,
I am the utter contempt of my neighbors
and an object of dread to my closest friends—
those who see me on the street flee from me.
12 I am forgotten as though I were dead;
I have become like broken pottery.
13 For I hear many whispering,
"Terror on every side!"
They conspire against me
and plot to take my life.
14 But I trust in you, LORD;
I say, "You are my God."
15 My times are in your hands;
deliver me from the hands of my enemies,
from those who pursue me.
16 Let your face shine on your servant;
save me in your unfailing love.
17 Let me not be put to shame, LORD,
for I have cried out to you;
but let the wicked be put to shame
and be silent in the realm of the dead.
18 Let their lying lips be silenced,
for with pride and contempt
they speak arrogantly against the righteous.
19 How abundant are the good things
that you have stored up for those who fear you,
that you bestow in the sight of all,
on those who take refuge in you.
20 In the shelter of your presence you hide them
from all human intrigues;
you keep them safe in your dwelling
from accusing tongues.
21 Praise be to the LORD,
for he showed me the wonders of his love
when I was in a city under siege.
22 In my alarm I said,
"I am cut off from your sight!"
Yet you heard my cry for mercy
when I called to you for help.
23 Love the LORD, all his faithful people!
The LORD preserves those who are true to him,
but the proud he pays back in full.
24 Be strong and take heart,
all you who hope in the LORD.

DAY 24

Hope in the Waiting

For the woman who is continuing to pray even when her circumstances haven't changed.

SHAE HILL AND LYLI DUNBAR

TODAY'S READING: Psalm 31

MAJOR MOMENT: David kept praying to God even when his prayers remained unanswered.

KEY VERSE: Psalm 31:24
Be strong and take heart, all you who hope in the LORD.

In Psalm 31, we find David not just in present suffering but in prolonged suffering: Whatever he was praying for, the deliverance had not yet come to pass.

Can you relate? The painful aspect of prayers of supplication is the inevitable reality of waiting. Waiting for answers. Waiting for direction. Waiting for healing. Waiting for change.

In Psalm 31:9-13, what kind of waiting experience did David describe?

David's condition could be compared to what we find in the book of Job. His affliction was multilayered:

PHYSICAL
"My strength fails … and my bones grow weak." (v. 10)

EMOTIONAL
"I am in distress; my eyes grow weak with sorrow." (v. 9)
"Terror on every side!" (v. 13)

SOCIAL
"I am the utter contempt of my neighbors and an object of dread to my closest friends—those who see me on the street flee from me." (v. 11)

MORTAL
"[They] plot to take my life." (v. 13)

SPIRITUAL
"because of my affliction …" (v. 10)

How do you relate to what David is saying?

Have you experienced a time when waiting felt painful?

In his raw humanity, David relates to us. But by the power of the Holy Spirit, he leads us. After he cried out in his hurt, David said, *"But I trust in you, LORD; I say, 'You are my God.' My times are in your hands"* (Psalm 31:14-15).

David was hard pressed on all sides, but he was still pressing in spiritually, committed to God's will above all else. He said, *"Into your hands I commit my spirit"* (Psalm 31:5). These same words were later said by Jesus on the cross: *"Jesus called out with a loud voice, "Father, into your hands I commit my spirit." When he had said this, he breathed his last"* (Luke 23:46). Focused on the Father's will, Jesus remained silent as the wicked schemes of the enemy unfolded. As He faced His accusers, Christ persevered through the torment without retaliating, all to secure our redemption (1 Peter 2:22-24).

> Why is it challenging to commit our spirits to God and place our trust and our times into His hands?

David and Jesus' words show us both surrender and submission to God and His will. But surrender and submission grow increasingly difficult as we face difficult circumstances over a long period of time.

The longer we pray without seeing God's intervention ...
The longer we see our realities moving further from what we desire ...
The longer we cry out, doubting whether God hears us ...

This is why we must remember the humanity in the Bible. David understood the pain of life. Yet his closing words in Psalm 31:24 charge us: *"Be strong and take heart, all you who hope in the LORD!"*

Friend, as you wait on the Lord to answer the cries of your heart, may you be strengthened by Him, and may you be filled with courage. For *"after you have suffered a little while, will himself restore you and make you strong, firm and steadfast"* (1 Peter 5:10). We have an eternal hope because of His obedience. The resurrected Christ is seated in heaven at the right hand of the Father, waiting for the Day of Judgment when His enemies will be defeated (Hebrews 10:12-13). We, too, wait with hope, looking forward to the glory to come when He finally returns to deliver us from sin and suffering (Romans 8:16-25).

As we suffer, we can be reminded of and encouraged by other champions of the faith, like David — and most of all, Jesus Himself — who understand the toll of the human experience.

> What would it look like for you to *"be strong and take heart"* (Psalm 31:24) when you're waiting on God to answer you?

PRAYER PRACTICE

Heavenly Father, I know You see my every moment. You see every struggle I'm walking through, every question I'm asking, every bit of confusion I'm trying to understand, every prayer I'm crying out. God, it is so painful to wait sometimes. My heart and mind are tired. But I pray today that You would strengthen my spirit — that I would grow in grace and trust in You. Please help me not to get caught up in things I can't control, and help me redirect my thoughts to You, the maker of heaven and earth, the One who is sovereign over everything. I trust that You know every aching desire of my heart, and what is according to Your will is what will come to pass in due time. Thank You for always listening to me. I know I can come to You with anything. While I wait ... I pray this time will be marked by closeness with You. In Jesus' name, amen.

A song of ascents.

1 I lift up my eyes to the mountains—
where does my help come from?
2 My help comes from the LORD,
the Maker of heaven and earth.

3 He will not let your foot slip—
he who watches over you will not slumber;
4 indeed, he who watches over Israel
will neither slumber nor sleep.

5 The LORD watches over you—
the LORD is your shade at your right hand;
6 the sun will not harm you by day,
nor the moon by night.

7 The LORD will keep you from all harm—
he will watch over your life;
8 the LORD will watch over your coming and going
both now and forevermore.

DAY 25

Always Watching Over Us

For the woman who is placing her hope in the helping hands of God.

SHAE HILL AND ERICA WIGGENHORN

TODAY'S READING: Psalm 121

MAJOR MOMENT: A psalmist described God as our Helper in everything we're facing.

KEY VERSES: Psalm 121:7-8

The LORD will keep you from all harm—he will watch over your life; the LORD will watch over your coming and going both now and forevermore.

To wrap up our week, let's look at one last psalm: Psalm 121. Read the psalm below, along with the notes and questions we've included alongside it, and consider how it relates to what we've studied this week. Feel free to add your own notes, underlining and highlighting! Let's deeply dig into the text to discover all God wants to teach us about prayer through these words.

PSALM 121	NOTES
A song of ascents.	
1 I lift up my eyes to the mountains— where does my help come from?	*Look up! Eyes up! Off my circumstances and on my God!*
2 My help comes from the LORD, the Maker of heaven and earth.	*The same God who MADE the heavens and earth is listening to my prayers!*
3 He will not let your foot slip— he who watches over you will not slumber; 4 indeed, he who watches over Israel will neither slumber nor sleep.	*God is always listening. He doesn't retreat or take breaks. He is constant.*
5 The LORD watches over you— the LORD is your shade at your right hand;	

6 the sun will not harm you by day,
  nor the moon by night.

7 The LORD will keep you from all harm—
  he will watch over your life;
8 the LORD will watch over your coming and going
  both now and forevermore.

See Psalm 91.

Wherever I am, wherever I go, whatever my circumstances may be, the Lord watches over it all.

REFLECTION QUESTIONS

1. In every supplication you bring the Lord today, how can you see Him as your Helper? (Psalm 121:1-2)

2. Look at Psalm 121:4. How do these words encourage you, especially in a time where God may feel quiet or even absent?

PRAYER PRACTICE

Write a prayer below, placing in the hands of God everything you hope for and earnestly ask for.

WEEK FIVE

WEEKEND REFLECTION

As we conclude our week focusing on prayers of supplication, there is something we must acknowledge and create space to process: *grief.*

Chances are, as you are going through this study guide, you carry grief inside of you from these two scenarios:

1. You have been praying for an answer or solution in one area for a long time without seeing change.
2. In the past, you prayed about something important to you, and what happened in the end was the opposite of the result you were hoping for.

Friend, if this is true for you, the heartbreak you carry is real and is not ignored. God sees the grief you carry in your weary heart. It's OK to acknowledge that you have experienced or are currently experiencing disappointment in your prayer life. Remember: You can talk to God about anything.

As you continue to press in to these psalms and teachings, cling to the words of Lamentations 3:21-26:

Yet this I call to mind and therefore I have hope: Because of the LORD's great love we are not consumed, for his compassions never fail. They are new every morning; great is your faithfulness. I say to myself, "The LORD is my portion; therefore I will wait for him." The LORD is good to those whose hope is in him, to the soul who seeks him; it is good to wait quietly for the salvation of the LORD.

Even though there are parts of our stories where we carry grief, we can still have hope. God cares for us tenderly in our grief and through the tears we cry. Take a few moments to journal about some of the grief you may have experienced as you process past prayer requests that have gone seemingly unanswered. Before you journal, receive this prayer:

A PRAYER FOR YOU

Father God, I know I am not hidden from You. You are close to me. As I think about prayer requests from my past that still linger with disappointment and grief because of their outcomes, I know You are close to me even here. I am making space today to grieve what needs to be grieved, process what needs to be processed, cry the tears I need to cry. But I will not let this grief create a wedge between You and me. I know You always have eventual, eternal good in mind, so I am choosing to trust You with all the details of situations I'm in. With every prayer request I bring to You. With everything that weighs heavily on my heart. Remind me that the lack of answers, change or intervention from You is not a punishment or a result of You ignoring me. I know You love me. I know You see me. I know You hear my every plea. I love You, Lord. Allow healing to take place as I continue to process these emotions. In Jesus' name, amen.

Though we've studied it this week as a prayer of supplication, Church tradition has labeled Psalm 143 the last of the seven "penitential psalms." *What does that mean?*

The seven penitential psalms, sometimes called "psalms of confession," include Psalm 6, Psalm 32, Psalm 38, Psalm 51, Psalm 102, Psalm 130 and Psalm 143. In each, the psalmist recognizes his sin and his need for God's forgiveness. For example, Psalm 51 chronicles David's anguish after his sin against Bathsheba, and Psalm 32 shares the joy of his forgiveness. As such, these psalms form a helpful collection of prayers to acknowledge the nature of sin and the importance of repentance. In fact, the early Church may have used Psalm 51, also known as "The Sinner's Guide," at the closing of each morning service.

Scholars disagree on exactly when the "penitential psalm" designation came about. It might have started with Origen in the third century or Augustine in the fifth century. Over the years, however, it became popular to review and reflect on these psalms during Lent (a season some Christians observe for 40 days before Easter). We still see this practice in some church traditions, and these psalms have much to teach us all!

WEEK SIX

PRAYERS OF INTERCESSION

1 Praise the LORD.
Give thanks to the LORD, for he is good;
his love endures forever.
2 Who can proclaim the mighty acts of the LORD
or fully declare his praise?
3 Blessed are those who act justly,
who always do what is right.
4 Remember me, LORD, when you show favor to your people,
come to my aid when you save them,
5 that I may enjoy the prosperity of your chosen ones,
that I may share in the joy of your nation
and join your inheritance in giving praise.
6 We have sinned, even as our ancestors did;
we have done wrong and acted wickedly.
7 When our ancestors were in Egypt,
they gave no thought to your miracles;
they did not remember your many kindnesses,
and they rebelled by the sea, the Red Sea.
8 Yet he saved them for his name's sake,
to make his mighty power known.
9 He rebuked the Red Sea, and it dried up;
he led them through the depths as through a desert.
10 He saved them from the hand of the foe;
from the hand of the enemy he redeemed them.
11 The waters covered their adversaries;
not one of them survived.
12 Then they believed his promises
and sang his praise.
13 But they soon forgot what he had done
and did not wait for his plan to unfold.
14 In the desert they gave in to their craving;
in the wilderness they put God to the test.
15 So he gave them what they asked for,
but sent a wasting disease among them.
16 In the camp they grew envious of Moses
and of Aaron, who was consecrated to the LORD.
17 The earth opened up and swallowed Dathan;
it buried the company of Abiram.
18 Fire blazed among their followers;
a flame consumed the wicked.
19 At Horeb they made a calf
and worshiped an idol cast from metal.
20 They exchanged their glorious God
for an image of a bull, which eats grass.
21 They forgot the God who saved them,
who had done great things in Egypt,
22 miracles in the land of Ham
and awesome deeds by the Red Sea.
23 So he said he would destroy them—
had not Moses, his chosen one,
stood in the breach before him
to keep his wrath from destroying them.
24 Then they despised the pleasant land;
they did not believe his promise.
25 They grumbled in their tents
and did not obey the LORD.

[26] So he swore to them with uplifted hand
that he would make them fall in the wilderness,
[27] make their descendants fall among the nations
and scatter them throughout the lands.
[28] They yoked themselves to the Baal of Peor
and ate sacrifices offered to lifeless gods;
[29] they aroused the LORD's anger by their wicked deeds,
and a plague broke out among them.
[30] But Phinehas stood up and intervened,
and the plague was checked.
[31] This was credited to him as righteousness
for endless generations to come.
[32] By the waters of Meribah they angered the LORD,
and trouble came to Moses because of them;
[33] for they rebelled against the Spirit of God,
and rash words came from Moses' lips.
[34] They did not destroy the peoples
as the LORD had commanded them,
[35] but they mingled with the nations
and adopted their customs.
[36] They worshiped their idols,
which became a snare to them.
[37] They sacrificed their sons
and their daughters to false gods.
[38] They shed innocent blood,
the blood of their sons and daughters,
whom they sacrificed to the idols of Canaan,
and the land was desecrated by their blood.
[39] They defiled themselves by what they did;
by their deeds they prostituted themselves.
[40] Therefore the LORD was angry with his people
and abhorred his inheritance.
[41] He gave them into the hands of the nations,
and their foes ruled over them.
[42] Their enemies oppressed them
and subjected them to their power.
[43] Many times he delivered them,
but they were bent on rebellion
and they wasted away in their sin.
[44] Yet he took note of their distress
when he heard their cry;
[45] for their sake he remembered his covenant
and out of his great love he relented.
[46] He caused all who held them captive
to show them mercy.
[47] Save us, LORD our God,
and gather us from the nations,
that we may give thanks to your holy name
and glory in your praise.
[48] Praise be to the LORD, the God of Israel,
from everlasting to everlasting.
Let all the people say, "Amen!"
Praise the LORD.

DAY 26

Speak for Me

For the woman who needs the reminder that redemption is always possible.

MICHAELA ROSCOE AND SARAH FRAZER

TODAY'S READING: Psalm 106

MAJOR MOMENT: A psalmist reflected on Israel's rebellion against the Lord and highlighted God's mercy toward them.

KEY VERSE: Psalm 106:23
So he said he would destroy them—had not Moses, his chosen one, stood in the breach before him to keep his wrath from destroying them.

Have you ever wanted to pray for someone but had one of these thoughts?

- *How? Am I even qualified?*
- *Does the Lord care if I'm praying for others?*
- *What difference would it make if I pray or they pray?*
- *The Lord isn't even answering my prayers for myself, so why would He answer when I pray for someone else?*

If so, we pray this week's study gives you some reassurance that you aren't alone. As we approach the conclusion of this study, we are going to dive into another type of prayer central to the gospel and the heart of Jesus Himself: intercession.

First, what exactly *is* intercession? Well, we actually see intercession every day. Intercession simply means going between or acting on behalf of another person. For example: A lawyer intercedes with the court on behalf of his or her client. It means stepping up for those who need it (even if they don't know they do!). Prayerful intercession means approaching the Lord on someone's behalf.

Let's begin our week by looking at an intercessory prayer for a group of people: the nation of Israel. In Psalm 106, our psalmist asked the Lord to help and save Israel in their time of need. He begged for the Lord to remember them, or in other words, remember His promise to rescue them from their enemies.

Think of a group of people in your life who have not yet experienced deliverance from sin, or a group of people you care for who are widely suffering or rebelling. Is it your nation, community, co-workers, friends? Write it down below and keep this in mind as we move through today's psalm and corresponding questions.

Before he spoke his plea, the writer of Psalm 106 delved into Israel's history in verses 6-46.

Write down some of the sins you see the psalmist confessing on behalf of his nation. When you reflect on the history of the people you want to pray for today, what sin or greatest need comes to mind? (You may consider your own sin as well.)

Write down some of the actions God performed for Israel, as recorded in Psalm 106. How have you seen God at work in the history of the people you want to pray for today?

Our history greatly informs our present. Reflecting on what we have experienced individually or communally can be difficult, but the ways the Lord has delivered us bring us toward praise!

Psalm 106:40-48 indicates this psalm was composed at the end of Israel's Babylonian exile (remember this from Days 14 and 16?) — but not yet at their deliverance. The Israelites were experiencing great hardship, but the psalmist did not overlook that God had already begun to have mercy on them. Though they were still experiencing persecution, the psalmist reflected on the goodness of the Lord and asked boldly in faith for Him to save Israel from captivity.

Read Ephesians 2:4-5. Why does God act mercifully toward us, just as He acted mercifully toward Israel? (Psalm 106:45)

Finally, the psalmist made his request. He cried out to God, much as you and I do when we have reached the end of ourselves. Let's face it: The psalmist couldn't control the actions of a nation, just as we can't control the choices of any group.

We cannot control any habitual sin patterns or widespread rebellion against the Lord.
We cannot change the hearts of people to repent from their sin.
We can't even persuade them to see their sin as sin.

But the psalmist asked the Lord for forgiveness and deliverance *anyway*. And we can plead for the Lord to change people's hearts (including ours) and grant mercy.

It takes faith to believe that the Lord is merciful and true to His Word and that Jesus loves our broken, sinful communities. We can step in boldly with this faith to pray for our friends, families or whole nations to repent and be delivered from sin, just as we have been delivered by Christ.

The Psalm 106 psalmist spent most of this prayer reflecting on the past. But in verses 47-48 he projected into the future.

> What did the psalmist ask of the Lord, and what did he say he would *"give"*? How does this example inspire your own prayer?

Spoiler alert: The Lord DID deliver the Israelites and return them to their land. (Ezra 1:1-4; Ezra 5:13-15) What a merciful God!

PRAYER PRACTICE

Jesus told us in his final summation command, *"Love the Lord your God with all your heart and with all your soul and with all your mind and with all your strength.' The second is this: 'Love your neighbor as yourself.' There is no commandment greater than these"* (Mark 12:30–31).

Begin your prayer practice this week asking the Holy Spirit to reveal any one in your life you could intercede for in prayer.

Jesus Christ & The Holy Spirit: *The Great Intercessors*

Sometimes we feel like we don't always have the best words to offer the Lord. When we feel this way, it might cross our minds ... *Why should I pray for others?* It's a great question, with a simple answer: As believers, we intercede for others because Christ intercedes for us and has given us the Holy Spirit to help us pray. We are not powerless in Christ. Also, the Lord truly wants us to pray on behalf of others. Let's look at how this is true.

JESUS

"My dear children, I write this to you so that you will not sin. But if anybody does sin, we have an ***advocate*** *with the Father—Jesus Christ, the Righteous One."* (1 John 2:1, emphasis added)

"Therefore he is able to save completely those who come to God through him, because he always lives to ***intercede*** *for them."* (Hebrews 7:25, emphasis added)

"Who then is the one who condemns? No one. Christ Jesus who died—more than that, who was raised to life—is at the right hand of God and is also ***interceding*** *for us."* (Romans 8:34, emphasis added)

Charles Spurgeon says, "He seems to have thought of all [His people's] wants, of all their needs, of all their weaknesses, and in one long stream of intercession, he pours out his heart before his Father's throne."[1] What an advocate! Not only is Jesus petitioning on our behalf, but He also took on the punishment we sinfully deserved.

Without the intervention and advocacy of Christ, we would not have the gospel. Intercession is God's idea and Jesus' mission. It is a great blessing to be able to advocate for others just like Jesus does for us. By prayerfully interceding, we are becoming more like Christ.

THE HOLY SPIRIT

When God the Father sent the Holy Spirit after Jesus' ascension, (John 14:26; Acts 2) He gave us power for prayer. In intercessory prayer, we can have confidence that the Spirit is working and moving in us, and the Spirit is also praying for us.

"In the same way, the Spirit helps us in our weakness. We do not know what we ought to pray for, but the Spirit himself ***intercedes*** *for us through wordless groans. And he who searches our hearts knows the mind of the Spirit, because the Spirit* ***intercedes*** *for God's people in accordance with the will of God."* (Romans 8:26-27, emphases added)

Before you pray, remember you have the Spirit. Ask Him to form and empower your prayers.

Think on this quote from Spurgeon as you spend time praying for others this week: "I pray you use it [intercessory prayer] on the behalf of the poor, the sick, the afflicted, the tempted, the tried, the desponding, the despairing; when thou hast the King's ear, speak to him for us."[2]

PSALM 60

For the director of music. To the tune of "The Lily of the Covenant." A miktam of David. For teaching. When he fought Aram Naharaim and Aram Zobah, and when Joab returned and struck down twelve thousand Edomites in the Valley of Salt.

1 You have rejected us, God, and burst upon us;
you have been angry—now restore us!
2 You have shaken the land and torn it open;
mend its fractures, for it is quaking.
3 You have shown your people desperate times;
you have given us wine that makes us stagger.
4 But for those who fear you, you have raised a banner
to be unfurled against the bow.
5 Save us and help us with your right hand,
that those you love may be delivered.
6 God has spoken from his sanctuary:
"In triumph I will parcel out Shechem
and measure off the Valley of Sukkoth.
7 Gilead is mine, and Manasseh is mine;
Ephraim is my helmet,
Judah is my scepter.
8 Moab is my washbasin,
on Edom I toss my sandal;
over Philistia I shout in triumph."
9 Who will bring me to the fortified city?
Who will lead me to Edom?
10 Is it not you, God, you who have now rejected us
and no longer go out with our armies?
11 Give us aid against the enemy,
for human help is worthless.
12 With God we will gain the victory,
and he will trample down our enemies.

DAY 27

Lord, Help Those I Love!

For the woman who needs God to do what she can't do for the people she loves.

MICHAELA ROSCOE AND JOY A. WILLIAMS

TODAY'S READING: Psalm 60

MAJOR MOMENT: David recalled that human salvation is vain, but God is a valiant Savior.

KEY VERSE: Psalm 60:11
Give us aid against the enemy, for human help is worthless.

How often do you feel like you've tried and tried to help a loved one with something they're struggling with, but nothing you do is working?

Loved ones living with depression, family members struggling with addiction, rebellious children, or people who you just don't understand why they're doing what they are ... No matter how much you talk to them, how many resources you provide, it seems like nothing is helping.

That feeling is hollowing.

However, here's some really good news: You can't do it. But Jesus can. You are free from the pressure of saving someone from their hardship. **Savior is a role only Jesus can fulfill; He provides true healing and restoration.**

We find an example of this holy surrender in Psalm 60, which is set in a time of hardship for the psalmist, King David. He used this prayer to reflect on how broken he and his people felt but also to reflect on the victory God had given him in many battles.

> Look at verses 1-10. Write down some emotions David may have been feeling. (This will take some interpretation: For example, in verse 9, you could say David felt lost or directionless.)

David was a beloved king chosen by God for God's purposes. Yet even David, who was anointed by the Spirit of the Lord, (1 Samuel 16:13) sometimes felt like he was alone and failing at helping his people.

What is significant is what came next.

Read Psalm 60:11 and fill in the blanks: *"Give us aid against the enemy, for* __________ __________ *is* __________________ *."*

Let's get *really honest* with ourselves. In what areas of life have you been relying on human power to save you instead of God's power?

David called human salvation *"worthless"* In other words: futile, useless, without value. If our pride gets involved, this truth about our efforts can actually hurt a bit. But in light of the gospel, it is so sweet. Second Corinthians 12:9 says Christ's power is *"made perfect"* in our weakness. It is actually good that we cannot save others! We can bring God glory as He delivers those around us.

Psalm 60:12 says, *"With God we will gain the victory, and he will trample down our enemies."* The ESV translation uses the phrasing *"we shall do valiantly."* To be valiant means to act bravely or courageously.

Friend, it's time to trade in vanity for valiance.

We have such a deep desire to help our loved ones that it can be hard to relinquish control to God ... but God wants to tread down their foes and ours. Let's surrender to Him.

Use the lines on the left to list people and situations you have been holding on to too tightly. What or who have you been trying to save on your own? On the right side, write "belongs to God" as a symbol of handing over each person and situation to Him. (We've completed one set of lines for you as an example below.)

THE HEALTH OF MY CHILDREN	BELONGS TO GOD

Let's wrap up the day with the words of theologian Matthew Henry: "Oh, that we would learn to just trust in God; call upon Him for our help. Rather than looking to man, look to God.... It is a great day when I just yield to God all the issues of my life. And I trust Him completely."[1]

PRAYER PRACTICE

Spend some time praying through the list you made above, where you traded in your vanity for valiance in God.

As David asked God to *"Save us and help us with your right hand"* (Psalm 60:5), his prayer pointed to God's power. It also prophetically pointed to the work of God's Son, Jesus, who is sitting at His right hand in heaven today.

Return to the list you made yesterday (Day 26). Pray verses 4-5, 11-12 over the needs of those on your list.

For the director of music. A psalm of David.

1 May the LORD answer you when you are in distress;
may the name of the God of Jacob protect you.
2 May he send you help from the sanctuary
and grant you support from Zion.
3 May he remember all your sacrifices
and accept your burnt offerings.
4 May he give you the desire of your heart
and make all your plans succeed.
5 May we shout for joy over your victory
and lift up our banners in the name of our God.
May the LORD grant all your requests.
6 Now this I know:
The LORD gives victory to his anointed.
He answers him from his heavenly sanctuary
with the victorious power of his right hand.
7 Some trust in chariots and some in horses,
but we trust in the name of the LORD our God.
8 They are brought to their knees and fall,
but we rise up and stand firm.
9 LORD, give victory to the king!
Answer us when we call!

DAY 28

Send Help, Lord

For the woman whose loved ones are facing a battle.

MICHAELA ROSCOE AND JODIE NIZNIK

TODAY'S READING: Psalm 20

MAJOR MOMENT: A psalmist asked God to answer, help and remember His people in their trouble.

KEY VERSE: Psalm 20:2
May he send you help from the sanctuary
and grant you support from Zion.

When we're praying for someone who is suffering, our prayers can feel desperate and conflicted. We may be full of hope but also experience despair and frustration while we wait for the Lord to intervene. Sometimes, we even find ourselves on our knees *begging* for the Lord to do something.

In Psalm 20, the nation of Israel felt compelled to pray for King David as he prepared to ride into battle. This psalm is what they prayed.

Imagine King David at the tabernacle of God, offering sacrifices to prepare for battle when he heard the people call out, *"May the LORD answer you when you are in distress"* (v. 1). Theologian Derek Kidner says this is "one of the most stirring of the Psalms, by its tense awareness of life-and-death issues soon to be resolved."[1]

You may feel this same awareness when your friends are struggling and desperately need you to pray for them.

> Read Psalm 20 in full, and then focus on verse 1. What is *"distress[ing]"* for your loved ones today?

Read verses 1-5. What is the first word of every single one of these verses?

How many times is this word used throughout the psalm?

The Hebrew root word used here in the phrase *"**May** the LORD **answer**"* (v. 1) is עָנָה (anah). It means to testify, to hear, to sing, to shout, to give account, to beg God to heed and answer.[2] The verb form here is called "imperfective," which means it also could be translated "may He pay attention" or "may He respond." When Israel prayed, *"**May** the LORD answer ..."* they were fervently asking the Lord to hear them and answer their prayers because they greatly cared for the one they prayed for.

Isn't this familiar? Psalm 20 gives us an example of how to come before God and pray for a loved one who needs Him — with conviction that He is listening. It's as if the people were believing in a promise God had given, though it hadn't been fulfilled yet.

When you come to the Lord in prayer for those who you know are facing a battle, consider praying this very psalm for them.

Using verses 1-3, complete the corresponding "may" statements. We can use this as a guideline for our prayers.

1. *"May the LORD ________________ __________ when you are in ______________..."* (v. 1a)
2. *"May he send you ______________ from the ___________________ ..."* (v. 2a)
3. *"May he remember__________ ______________ ____________________ ..."* (v. 3)

Below are some blank "may" statements. Use these lines to write down how your loved ones need deliverance. When you approach the throne of God to petition for them, what are you specifically praying for?

1. May the Lord ____.
2. May He send ____.
3. May He remember ____.

Finally, here are three more blank "may" statements. Use these to think of how YOU need deliverance. How would you like a friend to be praying for you in your day of trouble? Consider asking a trusted friend or family member to pray for you based on these lines.

1. May the Lord ______________________________.
2. May He send ______________________________.
3. May He remember ______________________________.

In the midst of great petition and making requests of the Lord, the psalmist(s) also took a moment to recognize the character of God as strong, merciful and greatly desiring good for His people. (vv. 6-8) This is our God!

A closer look at this psalm also shows that the psalmist didn't prescribe how God **should** rescue the king and those headed into battle, but he asked open-handedly that God **would** answer, send help, and remember His people in their trouble (Psalm 20:2-3). This is a prayer we, too, can pray with assurance because we trust God to answer as the loving Father He is (Matthew 7:9-11).

We won't ever know the full extent of God's plans and purposes for our loved ones or ourselves. But with Jesus as our example, we can trust that our good God only acts in love (1 John 4:8-10).

PRAYER PRACTICE

Return to the exercise above and turn the three statements for your loved ones into specific prayers for each person on your list of those in need of intercession this week. If you do not have anyone to pray for yet, or are not sure who to pray for, pause before praying and ask the Holy Spirit to bring a name or a circumstance to mind. Then, begin here and add your three statements like below:

Lord, I know You see the hearts of my loved ones who are facing a battle, and You love them more than I can imagine — just as You love me more than I can imagine. Lord, may you ______________________. May you send ______________________. Lord, remember ______________________.

INTERCESSORS THROUGHOUT THE BIBLE

COMPLETE THE FOLLOWING CHART TO OBSERVE DIFFERENT BIBLICAL FIGURES PRAYERFULLY INTERCEDING AND HOW GOD RESPONDED TO THIS.

VERSES	WHO INTERCEDED?	WHO DID THEY PRAY FOR?	HOW DID GOD RESPOND?
Genesis 17:17-22			
Numbers 14:11-22			
Job 42:7-12			
Job 42:7-12			
John 11:38-44			

Of David.

[1] To you, LORD, I call;
you are my Rock,
do not turn a deaf ear to me.
For if you remain silent,
I will be like those who go down to the pit.
[2] Hear my cry for mercy
as I call to you for help,
as I lift up my hands
toward your Most Holy Place.
[3] Do not drag me away with the wicked,
with those who do evil,
who speak cordially with their neighbors
but harbor malice in their hearts.
[4] Repay them for their deeds
and for their evil work;
repay them for what their hands have done
and bring back on them what they deserve.
[5] Because they have no regard for the deeds
of the LORD
and what his hands have done,
he will tear them down
and never build them up again.
[6] Praise be to the LORD,
for he has heard my cry for mercy.
[7] The LORD is my strength and my shield;
my heart trusts in him, and he helps me.
My heart leaps for joy,
and with my song I praise him.
[8] The LORD is the strength of his people,
a fortress of salvation for his anointed one.
[9] Save your people and bless your inheri-
tance;
be their shepherd and carry them forever.

DAY 29

Confidence in God's Character

For the woman who needs confidence
that the Lord will carry her and her people.

MICHAELA ROSCOE AND TRISHA HAWK

TODAY'S READING: Psalm 28

MAJOR MOMENT: David prayed for God to be his people's shield and shepherd.

KEY VERSE: Psalm 28:9
Save your people and bless your inheritance;
be their shepherd and carry them forever.

Sometimes, doubt shows up like an unwanted companion. We doubt that our friends will stick with us in hardship. We doubt that someone close to us is going to keep their word. We doubt that our efforts as parents are going to be fruitful. The worst part is … sometimes these doubts become a heartbreaking reality.

And then it's just a little easier to doubt that God is listening when we pray. Or doubt that God is who He says He is. Or doubt that the Lord will carry us through hardship. When we let doubt into our hearts, it is easy to think: OK, I'll pray, but I doubt God is going to help me or those I'm praying for.

When doubt creeps in, it is easy to forget who God is and why we can trust Him. But in the midst of prayer, especially prayer for others, evaluating the character of God and all He has done for us can remind us of the security we have in bringing our prayers to Him.

Psalm 28 reveals many characteristics of God through the recounting of His actions.

> In the chart on the following page, list the verses of this psalm that describe the characteristics of God.

The Lord is ...	Verses of Psalm 28 that show this: *(You can use the same verse more than once.)*
STRONG	
JUST	
MERCIFUL	
ATTENTIVE/LISTENING	
TRUSTWORTHY/FAITHFUL	

Let's consider these metaphors together and allow them to bolster our faith:

1. The Lord is our Rock (Psalm 28:1).

Throughout the Old Testament, the Hebrew word for "rock" symbolizes God's stability and faithfulness. In biblical times, rocky cliffs and caves commonly provided security from enemies; for example, David himself hid in a cave while King Saul pursued him (1 Samuel 22:1).

Have you ever stood on a rock at the pinnacle of a mountain, confident the rock would not move as you took in the view? In the same way, God is our Rock. When our circumstances are uncertain, His steady and faithful hand will hold us as we trust Him.

2. The Lord is our Shield (Psalm 28:7).

David's battle experience (2 Samuel 10:17; 1 Samuel 18:7) gave him insight into the necessity of a shield to protect him from swords and arrows. Likewise, God promises to be our Shield and protect us. Sometimes we see His protection; other times, He works in ways we cannot see (Isaiah 55:8-9). In seasons of hardship and struggle, we can take refuge in Him (Psalm 18:30).

3. The Lord is our Shepherd (Psalm 28:9).

As David ended his prayer, he shifted from personal prayer to intercession on behalf of his people, Israel: He asked the Lord to *"be their shepherd and carry them forever"* (Psalm 28:9b). David (once a shepherd himself) was familiar with the characteristics of a reliable shepherd. He understood a sheep's reliance on its shepherd for protection and provision. In asking God to be Israel's Shepherd, David affirmed their complete dependence on Him to meet their needs. As God's children today, we, too, can trust God's promise to provide everything we need (Philippians 4:19).

In Psalm 28, we see the Lord's character in action. In verses 7-8, David declared that he relied on the Lord's strength.

We, too, can confidently declare this:

"The LORD is my ______________________ and my ______________________; my heart ______________ in him, and he ______________ me. My heart leaps for joy, and with my song I ______________________ him" (v. 7).

In what areas of your life do you need the Lord's strength?

In what areas do the people around you need His strength?

When we trust God as our strength, we can have confidence He will help us. This may look different than what we ask or expect, but remember: The Lord is faithful to those He loves.

"The LORD is the ______________ of his people; a ______________ of ______________ for his anointed one." (v. 8)

Even if we are doubting, these truths affirm we have a good God who loves and helps us in our need.

My dear friend, if you can say, "The Lord is my strength," you can bear anything *and* everything. You could bear *a* martyr's death if the Lord should be your strength. He could make *a* stalk *of* wheat to bear up *the* whole world if he strengthened it.

CHARLES SPURGEON[1]

When we are praying for a loved one, community, enemy or anyone else, we need the Lord to sustain us *and* them. So David reminded himself of God's strength to orient his heart before making his request.

Finally, David stated his petition for the Lord to be his people's strength. This is a prayer for those who need the Lord's guidance and provision.

> Read Psalm 28:9. Who do you need to pray for who needs God to be their shepherd and carry them forever? Write down a few names.

We could add our own names to this list. If you are doubting the Lord's strength and provision for yourself and need prayerful intercession, send this psalm to a friend or family member and ask them to pray verse 9 over you as well.

PRAYER PRACTICE

Use the space below to write a prayer beginning with identifying who God is, then moving into prayer for those you listed above, asking God in His strength to shepherd and carry them forever.

[1] Sing joyfully to the LORD, you righteous;
it is fitting for the upright to praise him.
[2] Praise the LORD with the harp;
make music to him on the ten-stringed lyre.
[3] Sing to him a new song;
play skillfully, and shout for joy.
[4] For the word of the LORD is right and true;
he is faithful in all he does.
[5] The LORD loves righteousness and justice;
the earth is full of his unfailing love.
[6] By the word of the LORD the heavens were made,
their starry host by the breath of his mouth.
[7] He gathers the waters of the sea into jars;
he puts the deep into storehouses.
[8] Let all the earth fear the LORD;
let all the people of the world revere him.
[9] For he spoke, and it came to be;
he commanded, and it stood firm.
[10] The LORD foils the plans of the nations;
he thwarts the purposes of the peoples.
[11] But the plans of the LORD stand firm forever,
the purposes of his heart through all generations.
[12] Blessed is the nation whose God is the LORD,
the people he chose for his inheritance.
[13] From heaven the LORD looks down
and sees all mankind;
[14] from his dwelling place he watches
all who live on earth—
[15] he who forms the hearts of all,
who considers everything they do.
[16] No king is saved by the size of his army;
no warrior escapes by his great strength.
[17] A horse is a vain hope for deliverance;
despite all its great strength it cannot save.
[18] But the eyes of the LORD are on those who fear him,
on those whose hope is in his unfailing love,
[19] to deliver them from death
and keep them alive in famine.
[20] We wait in hope for the LORD;
he is our help and our shield.
[21] In him our hearts rejoice,
for we trust in his holy name.
[22] May your unfailing love be with us, LORD,
even as we put our hope in you.

DAY 30

Reasons To Celebrate

For the woman who wants to celebrate what God has done in her and her loved ones' lives.

MICHAELA ROSCOE AND KATY MCCOWN

TODAY'S READING: Psalm 33

MAJOR MOMENT: A psalmist celebrated God's past deliverance and trusted Him for present deliverance.

KEY VERSES: Psalm 33:4-5
For the word of the LORD is right and true; he is faithful in all he does.
The LORD loves righteousness and justice; the earth is full of his unfailing love.

You're at the end of this week and at the end of this study guide! Praise God for all the ways He has used your prayers over these six weeks! We will close our week of intercessory prayer by annotating Psalm 33. At the end of the psalm you'll find a couple reflection questions to guide your annotations if you'd like, or feel free to use the blank space to identify whatever it is you see in this psalm.

We've identified some important actions, characteristics of God, repeated words and **interesting images** in the text. What does this psalm make you think and feel?

PSALM 33

NOTES

1 Sing joyfully to the LORD, you righteous;
it is fitting for the upright to praise him.
2 Praise the LORD with the harp;
make music to him on the ten-stringed lyre.
3 Sing to him a new song;
play skillfully, and shout for joy.
4 For the word of the LORD is right and true;
he is faithful in all he does.
5 The LORD loves righteousness and justice;

NOTES

the earth is full of his unfailing love.
6 By the word of the Lord the heavens were made,
their starry host by the **breath of his mouth.**
7 **He gathers the waters of the sea into jars;**
he puts the deep into storehouses.
8 Let all the earth fear the Lord;
let all the people of the world revere him.
9 For he spoke, and it came to be;
he commanded, and it stood firm.
10 The Lord foils the plans of the nations;
he thwarts the purposes of the peoples.
11 But the plans of the Lord stand firm forever,
the purposes of his heart through all generations.
12 Blessed is the nation whose God is the Lord,
the people he chose for his inheritance.
13 From heaven the Lord looks down
and sees all mankind;
14 **from his dwelling place he watches**
all who live on earth—
15 **he who forms the hearts of all,**
who considers everything they do.
16 No king is saved by the size of his army;
no warrior escapes by his great strength.
17 A horse is a vain hope for deliverance;
despite all its great strength it cannot save.
18 But the eyes of the Lord are on those who fear him,
on those whose hope is in his unfailing love,
19 to deliver them from death
and keep them alive in famine.
20 We wait in hope for the Lord;
he is our help and our shield.
21 In him our hearts rejoice,
for we trust in his holy name.
22 May your unfailing love be with us, Lord,
even as we put our hope in you. (emphasis added)

REFLECTION QUESTIONS

What does this psalm instruct us to do as a result of God's goodness?

What characteristics or roles of God are described in this psalm?

Where is the intercessory prayer in this psalm?

PRAYER PRACTICE

Use the space below to write your continued prayer of intercession to the Lord using Psalm 33 as inspiration.

WEEK SIX

WEEKEND REFLECTION

Thank you for participating in this final week of our study of prayer through the book of Psalms. Wrapping up, let's turn our eyes toward Jesus and talk about what is true when we struggle to pray for others because we struggle to pray at all.

Friends, life can be hard — there is no getting around that. Sometimes in the midst of our own grief, lament, recovery, addiction or sinful patterns, we want to cry out in discouragement. We feel like we can't bring ourselves to pray for others because it is so hard even to pray for ourselves. We have nothing to give.

Remember this week when we looked at how Jesus and the Holy Spirit are great intercessors? (See page 183.) This truth is a great comfort when we feel this way.

There will be days where you need someone to intercede for **you**, but you lack the words to ask for help. On those days, remember these two things:

First, Jesus knows how you feel. He knows rejection, disappointment, ridicule, exhaustion, heartbreak, frustration, poverty, temptation and so much more. He knows your suffering. You are in the care of an empathetic God. The book of Hebrews reminds us of this:

"For we do not have a high priest who is unable to empathize with our weaknesses, but we have one who has been tempted in every way, just as we are—yet he did not sin." (Hebrews 4:15)

While the Lord loves for us to speak to Him and tell Him what is going on, even when our words fail, we can have confidence that He knows and cares.

Secondly, we can be confident that Christ is constantly interceding for us. He is bringing us back to Him. Remember the gospel, friends: Christ loves us so much that He became a man and sacrificed His very life so we could be united with Him. With a love that runs this deep, we can have confidence that He is speaking for us when we feel speechless. (Romans 8:34)

A PRAYER FOR YOU

Lord, thank You for the ways You've challenged, equipped and encouraged me in prayer throughout the past six weeks. Help me not to forget what I've learned, and prepare my heart for when I am emptied out and without words to pray. When I sit before You silent, broken and hollow, fill me with your comfort and peace. Jesus, You know my heart. You know my suffering. You have loved me despite my sin and washed me from it. So I pray for Your intercession today. You are the God of restoration. May You restore me and those around me. Bring us through our brokenness to Your glory. In Jesus' name, amen.

Praying *the* Lord's Prayer

In addition to studying the book of Psalms, we can also look to Matthew 6 for instruction from Jesus on how to pray. If you've been around Christian circles for a while, you may have heard this passage of Scripture called "the Lord's Prayer."

Jesus meant for this prayer to be used as a daily guide for how to converse with God — not in a way that's legalistic or just checks a box but as a guide for our benefit. It's what the human heart needs every day: communion with God.

THIS, THEN, IS HOW YOU SHOULD PRAY:

"'OUR FATHER IN HEAVEN,

HALLOWED BE YOUR NAME,

YOUR KINGDOM COME,

YOUR WILL BE DONE, ON EARTH AS IT IS IN HEAVEN.

GIVE US TODAY OUR DAILY BREAD.

AND FORGIVE US OUR DEBTS,

AS WE ALSO HAVE FORGIVEN OUR DEBTORS.

AND LEAD US NOT INTO TEMPTATION

BUT DELIVER US FROM THE EVIL ONE.'"

(MATTHEW 6:9-13)

Jesus' prayer lifts up God's will above His own. (v. 10) He establishes that the Lord will provide what we need daily. (v. 11) After that, He walks us through praying for forgiving hearts and the ability to stand against the temptations of the enemy. (vv. 12-13)

This is how we pray: In worship and thankfulness and praise, we ask for God's will, for what we need, for forgiveness, and for deliverance from evil.

We will readily admit we struggle to do this daily … and maybe that's the very reason why we can slip into spiritual funks so easily. So we created this guided prayer space for you to really experience the power of the Lord's Prayer. Use this as your safe space for learning, processing, journaling and communicating with your heavenly Father. Together, we can lean into what Jesus taught us through this perfect example of uncomplicated prayer — simple words spoken from a humble heart to a good God.

PRAY THEN LIKE THIS …

1. *"… Our Father in heaven, hallowed be your name."* (Matthew 6:9)

In the Old Testament, references to God as "Father" were limited and primarily used as an analogy rather than a personal name for God. So when Jesus addressed God as "our Father" in this prayer, His Israelite disciples would have been shocked by the relational intimacy. Calling God "our Father" is personal and opens the door for new understanding about our relationship with God. He isn't just our supreme authority; God is our heavenly Father.

God loves for us to draw near to Him and call out to Him as our Father. No matter what your relationship with your earthly father looks like, your heavenly Father wants a loving relationship with you. Friend, even though our hearts may get broken from the effects of sin on this side of eternity, God's goodness does not change. We must hold fast to the truth of who God is and His unchanging nature: He is a good Father.

PRAY

Use the space below to pray, worship and declare how personal and close God is to you as your Father. This will help you remember who is on the other side of your praying: The God who intricately made you, loved you from the start, and has good plans for your life. "Our Father" relieves the pressure we put on ourselves to "impress" (or at least avoid "failing") God in our prayers. You can pray to Him as a beloved daughter — not trying to win His affection but knowing He gives it to you freely.

2. *"Your kingdom come, your will be done, on earth as it is in heaven."* (Matthew 6:10)

The three sections here — *"your kingdom come," "your will be done"* and *"on earth as it is in heaven"* — are all wrapped up in a future promise. This means that as we pray, we look forward to the promise that awaits us: Jesus' return!

It's like sneaking into the kitchen while your mom makes dinner to "taste test" the meal. This advance taste sets our expectations and affirms our longing for the full meal promised to us. If we truly believe God's will is good and better than what we think we want right now, we won't reach for lesser things to temporarily satisfy us. If we know the meal will be so delicious and satisfying, we won't be nearly as tempted to fill up on candy bars in the minutes before the food is served.

However, this future promise comes with present responsibility for us to participate in God's Kingdom today. Why is this important? Because as we pray through this section, we are trading what we may want right now for God's will, which is always best in the long run. This prayer is our reminder that God's will is better than our short-term desires.

This is what it means for earth to be *"as it is in heaven."* We want to taste for ourselves His Kingdom that is to come. And we want to give others a taste as well through our lives of faithfulness, love and obedience to God.

PRAY

Before we pray through the things weighing on our hearts, let's journal and pray through God's agenda first — declaring that we want His will to be done in us and through us more than anything else. We want His will in every relationship and every area of our lives. When we trade our will for God's will, we are stepping into true surrender.

3. *"Give us today our daily bread."* (Matthew 6:11)

When Jesus taught us what to pray each day, His first request from God the Father was for daily bread. The Greek word for "daily," epiousion (ἐπιούσιον), can be best understood as referring to the present of today, here and now, as well as the days to come.

We see a variety of forms of bread in the Bible. In the Old Testament, it came as a loaf (Leviticus 2:4) and as manna from heaven. (Deuteronomy 8:3) Bread was a daily provision from God. (Exodus 16:4) But most importantly, in the New Testament, Jesus called Himself the Bread of Life. (John 6:35) And one day, God promises we will receive bread at the heavenly banquet. (Luke 22:16; Isaiah 25:6)

So the mention of bread in the Lord's Prayer is not just intended for us to pray in hopeful anticipation for the future (the heavenly banquet) but also to pray as we are sustained by God's perfect provision in the present (manna).

NOTE FROM JOEL

The image of bread in Scripture was developed even further by Jesus as He instituted Communion, (Luke 22:14–20) which reminds us of the Passover in the Old Testament. (Exodus 12:1–28) When we observe Communion today and break the bread, we are reminded of the body of Jesus — the One who sustains us, who redeemed us through the breaking of His own body.

As we read through the Bible, we can be on the lookout for other examples of images or ideas in the Old Testament that were shadows of something to come in the New Testament. The sacrificial system of an unblemished lamb, for instance, finds its fulfillment in Jesus, the Lamb of God, who is without sin yet took on the sin of humanity on the cross.

It can feel exhausting to rely on God's provision when it's just not coming yet ... when we've asked for a solution to our problems and our pain but we haven't seen the manna we want. But if God's provision isn't as we expected, then we must trust there's something God knows that we don't know. Even when what we see in front of us feels confusing. Even when what we see in front of us isn't at all what we thought it would look like. Even when we don't agree that this is good. We can trust Him.

PRAY

Use the space below to journal and pray through things you need, and even just desire, from God. And then trust Him for those answers in His perfect timing. Remember, friend, Jesus is the Bread of Life. He is the most miraculous provision and the One already given to us today.

4. *"and forgive us our debts, as we also have forgiven our debtors."* (Matthew 6:12)

For someone living during the time of Jesus, hearing the word "debt" would have stirred up many emotions. In those days, the weight of power within the government caused the overwhelming majority of people to be borrowers, not lenders. They knew what it was like to be under the burdensome weight of unpayable debt. What joy, what peace, what freedom, to know that Jesus had come to pay all their spiritual debt!

Even as Christians today, when we are reminded that we have been cleared of the debt of our sin because of the blood of Jesus Christ, it should cause us to jump for joy! And it should cause us to desire freedom and forgiveness for others too.

... Yes, even that person. You know, the one who used to be one of our closest friends, but now we feel an awkward distance. Or the one who spoke those cruel words that sometimes still replay in our heads at night. Or that family member we have a strained relationship with. However the word "forgiveness" makes you feel in light of hard relationships you may be facing, we understand. And so does Jesus.

Forgiving doesn't mean the wrong done is no longer wrong. Forgiving doesn't always mean everything is forgotten, like nothing ever happened. And you don't have to conquer the whole forgiveness journey today with that person. But today is a great opportunity to simply sit with the Lord and consider what forgiveness could look like. In this relationship. In your own heart. What would it look like to cooperate with the forgiveness Jesus has given to you and extend it to another person?

PRAY

Use the space below to thank God for the free gift of His forgiveness. As you consider anything you yourself need to confess and ask God to forgive, also ask God: Who is someone I need to forgive? Invite His help as you begin that process today.

5. *"And lead us not into temptation, but deliver us from the evil one."* (Matthew 6:13)

Temptation is a part of our human experience. Even Jesus was tempted. But before Jesus died, He promised the Holy Spirit would come to help us stand firm against the lure of sin. (John 14:25-27) So today, when we put our faith in Jesus, we are given the Holy Spirit to help us fight against our sin nature, the snares of the world and the designs of Satan.

Galatians 5:19-24 shows us that in our flesh, we would choose a life focused on ourselves: *"The acts of the flesh are obvious: sexual immorality, impurity and debauchery; idolatry and witchcraft; hatred, discord, jealousy, fits of rage, selfish ambition, dissensions, factions and envy; drunkenness, orgies, and the like. I warn you, as I did before, that those who live like this will not inherit the kingdom of God. But the fruit of the Spirit is love, joy, peace, forbearance, kindness, goodness, faithfulness, gentleness and self-control. Against such things there is no law. Those who belong to Christ Jesus have crucified the flesh with its passions and desires."*

Thanks to Jesus, we don't have to live as slaves to our sin.

PRAY

To close out the Lord's Prayer, pray from the place of victory we have as believers, and take your stand against the enemy. Spiritual warfare can seem like a complex or intimidating topic — but it doesn't have to paralyze our prayers. God hears us when we simply ask for His protection against temptation and the schemes of the evil one. We can trust Him to handle everything this means.

NOTES

NOTES

Appendix

Psalm 25 Acrostic Poem:
Psalm 25 is also an example of an acrostic poem, each verse beginning with a successive letter of the Hebrew alphabet. When Scripture was written in this acrostic format, it served as an aid in memorization.

In our English Bible translations, we can't see the original pattern since our alphabet is different from the Hebrew alphabet, but the idea is demonstrated below using paraphrased concepts from Psalm 25.

All the paths of the LORD are steadfast love and faithfulness
Be gracious to me and turn to me
Consider my affliction, my trouble, my foes
Deliver me
Eyes ever toward the LORD
Forgive all my sins
Guard my soul
He instructs sinners in the way, leading the humble in what is right
In You, my God, I trust
Join with David in confession
Keep God's covenant and His testimonies
Let me not be put to shame
Make me to know Your ways
None who wait for You shall be put to shame
Offspring shall inherit the land
Pardon my guilt, for it is great
Quiet my heart in trust
Remember Your mercy
Soul shall abide in well-being
Teach me Your paths
Upright and good is the LORD
Violent hatred my foes have for me
Who is the man who fears the LORD?
Exult over my enemies
You are the God of my salvation
Zeal of the LORD of hosts brings our Redeemer

Endnotes

WHAT IS PRAYER?

1. Hardin, Leslie T. "Prayer." *The Lexham Bible Dictionary,* Lexham Press, 2016.
2. Okholm, Dennis L. "Prayer." *Evangelical Dictionary of Biblical Theology,* Baker Reference Library. Baker Book House, 1996, p. 622.
3. Elwell, Walter A. and Barry J. Beitzel. "Prayer." *Baker Encyclopedia of the Bible,* Baker Book House, 1988, p. 1745.
4. Kapic, Kelly M. and Wesley Vander Lugt. *Pocket Dictionary of the Reformed Tradition,* The IVP Pocket Reference Series. IVP Academic, 2013, p. 88.
5. Hatchett, Randy. "Prayer." *Holman Illustrated Bible Dictionary,* Holman Bible Publishers, 2003, p. 1320.
6. Montgomery, James. "Prayer is the soul's sincere desire," hymn, 1818.

HOW TO BUILD A HABIT OF PRAYER

1. Graham, B. *Hope for the Troubled Heart.* Bantam Books, 1993, p. 146.

NOTES ON THE PSALMS

1. This information can be found through Logos Bible Software word lists and is based on the word counts in the original languages.
2. Athanasius of Alexandria (born c 296-298 BCE, died 373 CE) was the twentieth bishop of Alexandria, a Christian theologian, a church father, and the chief defender of Trinitarianism against the heresy of Ariansim.

Week One

DAY 1

1. Allen P. Ross, The Bible Knowledge Commentary: An Exposition of the Scriptures, 1985, 1, 895.

DAY 2

1. "Q. If the Milky Way was the size of a coffee cup, how big would the rest of the universe be?" National Aeronautics and Space Administration, edited by Nancy Bray, August 3, 2017, https://www.nasa.gov/centers/kennedy/about/information/science_faq.html.
2. Kid*ner, Derek. Psalms 1–72: An Introduction and* Commentary, InterVarsity Press, Downers Grove, IL, 1973.

Day 4

1. Kid*ner, Derek. Psalms 73–150: An Introduction and Commentary,* InterVarsity Press, Downers Grove, IL, 1975.

Week Two

DAY 8

1. Kidner, Derek. Qtd. in "Psalm 38." *The Enduring Word Bible Commentary* by David Guzik, 2020, https://enduringword.com/bible-commentary/psalm-38/.

Week Three

DAY 13

1. Baumol, Avi (2009). "Psalm 100: Mizmor l'Todah". *The Poetry of Prayer: Tehillim in Tefillah.* Gefen Publishing House Ltd.
2. Allen P. Ross, *The Bible Knowledge Commentary: Old Testament.* Colorado Springs: David C Cook, 1985, p. 865.

DAY 14

1. Allen P. Ross, *The Bible Knowledge Commentary: Old Testament.* Colorado Springs: David C Cook, 1985, p. 871.

DAY 15

1. Allen P. Ross, *The Bible Knowledge Commentary: Old Testament.* Colorado Springs: David C Cook, 1985, p. 891.

Week Four

DAY 16

1. Boga, Matt. "L(amen)ting with Hope." *The Gospel Coalition,* May 15, 2020. https://www.thegospelcoalition.org/article/lamenting-with-hope/

DAY 17

1. Brooks, Page and D. A. Neal. "Theodicy." *The Lexham Bible Dictionary,* Bellingham, WA, Lexham Press, 2016.
2. Horne, Thomas Hartwell. Cited in "Psalm 10 – From Times Of Trouble To Calm Confidence." *The Enduring Word Bible Commentary* by David Guzik, 2020. https://enduringword.com/bible-commentary/psalm-10/

DAY 18

1. Piper, John. "Death Rehearsal," excerpted from "I Have Kept the Faith," *desiringGod,* December 28, 1980. https://www.desiringgod.org/articles/death-rehearsal
2. Guzik, David. "Psalm 90 – The Prayer Of Moses In The Wilderness." *The Enduring Word Bible Commentary by David Guzik,* 2020. https://enduringword.com/bible-commentary/psalm-90/

DAY 19

1. Walter A. Elwell and Barry J. Beitzel, "Music and Musical Instruments," *Baker Encyclopedia of the Bible,* Grand Rapids, MI, Baker Book House, 1988. p. 1506.
2. Ramsey, K.J. "Scripture and Neuroscience Agree: It Helps to Lament in Community." *Christianity Today,* November 15, 2019. https://www.christianitytoday.com/ct/2019/november-web-only/neuroscience-and-scripture-agree-it-helps-to-lament-in-comm.html
3. Henry, Matthew. "Complete Commentary on Matthew 26." *Henry's Complete Commentary on the Whole Bible,* 1706, https://www.studylight.org/commentaries/mhm/psalms-60.html; Henry, Matthew. "Complete Commentary on Matthew 27." *Henry's Complete Commentary on the Whole Bible,* 1706, https://www.studylight.org/commentaries/eng/mhm/matthew-27.html.

WEEKEND REFLECTION

1. Nicoll, William R. "Commentary on Psalms 22." *The Expositor's Bible Commentary.* https://www.studylight.org/commentaries/eng/teb/psalms-22.html.

Week Five

DAY 21

1. Spurgeon, Charles. Cited in "Psalm 37 – Wisdom Over Worry." *The Enduring Word Bible Commentary by David Guzik,* 2020. https://enduringword.com/bible-commentary/psalm-37/

DAY 22

1. Boice, James Cameron. Cited in "Psalm 17 – Wisdom Over Worry." *The Enduring Word Bible Commentary by David Guzik,* 2020. https://enduringword.com/bible-commentary/psalm-17/

DAY 23

1. Spurgeon, Charles. Cited in "Psalm 143 – Hope for the Persecuted Soul." *The Enduring Word Bible Commentary by David Guzik,* 2020. https://enduringword.com/bible-commentary/psalm-143/

Week Six

JESUS CHRIST & THE HOLY SPIRIT: THE GREAT INTERCESSORS

1. Spurgeon, Charles. "Intercessory Prayer." *Metropolitan Tabernacle Pulpit Volume 7,* August 11, 1861. https://www.spurgeon.org/resource-library/sermons/intercessory-prayer-2/#flipbook/
2. Spurgeon, Charles. "Intercessory Prayer." *Metropolitan Tabernacle Pulpit Volume 7,* August 11, 1861. https://www.spurgeon.org/resource-library/sermons/intercessory-prayer-2/#flipbook/

DAY 27

1. Henry, Matthew. "Complete Commentary on Psalms 60:10." *Henry's Complete Commentary on the Whole Bible,* 1706, https://www.studylight.org/commentaries/mhm/psalms-60.html

DAY 28

1. Kidner, Derek. Cited in "Psalm 20 – The Lord Saves His Anointed." *The Enduring Word Bible Commentary by David Guzik,* 2020. https://enduringword.com/bible-commentary/psalm-20/
2. "ענו." *Brown-Driver-Briggs Hebrew and English Lexicon, Unabridged.* Electronic Database, Biblesoft, Inc., 2006. https://biblehub.com/hebrew/6030.htm

DAY 29

1. Spurgeon, Charles. "A Sacred Solo." *Spurgeon's Sermons Volume 24:* 1878, https://ccel.org/ccel/spurgeon/sermons24/sermons24.

ALSO AVAILABLE FROM

PROVERBS 31 MINISTRIES

40 DAYS THROUGH THE BIBLE

In this personal Bible study you will take a journey through the storyline of the Bible in 40 days so you can see major themes, how they are all connected and what that means for us as we read the Bible today. Discover the eight major things humanity longs for and how Jesus fulfills all of them for us, and stop the endless cycle of seeking and searching for satisfaction and find the answers to your deepest longings.

30 DAYS WITH JESUS

In *30 Days with Jesus: Experiencing His Presence Throughout the Old and New Testaments*, authors Lysa TerKeurst and Dr. Joel Muddamalle will help you come to understand that Jesus isn't hiding from us; He's waiting to be seen by us. You will experience His presence every single day learning to:

- Reframe your questions and doubts as opportunities to look for Jesus with greater intentionality throughout your day.
- Make connections between the Old and New Testaments so you can understand the Bible as one complete story.
- Overcome dread or confusion toward studying Scripture.

Proverbs 31
MINISTRIES

Know the Truth. Live the Truth. It changes everything.

If you were inspired by this study and desire to deepen your own personal relationship with Jesus Christ, Proverbs 31 Ministries has just what you are looking for.

Proverbs 31 Ministries exists to be a trusted friend who will take you by the hand and walk by your side, leading you one step closer to the heart of God through:

- Online daily devotions
- First 5 Bible study app
- Therapy and Theology Podcast
- Proverbs 31 Ministries Podcast
- COMPEL Pro Writers Training
- She Speaks Conference
- Biblical books and resources

Our desire is to help you to know the Truth and live the Truth. Because when you do, it changes everything.

For more information about Proverbs 31 Ministries, visit: www.Proverbs31.org.